Tipperary's Gift To China: Three Apostolic Lives, 1863-1898

Catholic Truth Society Of Ireland

Tipperary's Gift to China

THREE APOSTOLIC LIVES
(1863–1898)

NEW EDITION—ENLARGED

DUBLIN
CATHOLIC TRUTH SOCIETY OF IRELAND
24 UPPER O'CONNELL STREET · 1919

Tipperary's Gift to China

1.—SISTER ALICE O'SULLIVAN (Martyr).
In China, 1863-70.

2.—FATHER PATRICK MOLONEY, C.M.
In China, 1871-82.

3.—SISTER MARY VINCENT RYAN.
In China, 1882-98.

CONTENTS

FOREWORD

THE title of this little book sufficiently
explains its scope. It tells the story of
three Irish saintly and apostolic souls, who
had this in common, that they all sprang
from the soil of a single southern county,
and all, in succession, carried the Gospel
to far Cathay, at a period, not very distant,
when the Chinese Mission was practically
unknown in Ireland. There is also something remarkable in the chronological
continuity of their record. Only one year
after the Tien-tsin massacre of 1870, in
which Alice O'Sullivan won her martyr's
crown, Father Patrick Moloney arrived
at Kiang-si; and when in answer to his
call, his cousin, Mary Ryan, came out in
1882, she was grieved to learn that he had
just passed away in a lonely quest for
souls.

The history of the virgin-martyr is
based upon a biographical work by a

5

French Vincentian Father,* which has also been issued in a translation by Lady Herbert of Lea (Art and Book Co., 1900), and upon some articles in the *Irish Monthly*.† The account of Father Moloney and his cousin, which appeared first in *St. Joseph's Sheaf*, is based upon the recollections of friends, his own letters, and a memoir of his heroic death penned by his Bishop, Monseigneur Bray, C.M., Vicar Apostolic of Kiang-si.

---

* *Les Premières Martyrs de la Sainte-Enfance* (Paris, 1861).
† Vol. iv.

TIPPERARY'S GIFT TO CHINA

CHAPTER I

THE MARTYR OF CLONMEL

THIRTY years ago,* when the shadow of a terrible war had not yet darkened the Third Empire, and the fair land of France was still free from the horrors of bitter strife, Tien-tsin came suddenly before the world as the scene of a most awful massacre, by Chinese pagan rabble, of ten daughters of St. Vincent de Paul. The one thought on earth of these saintly and charitable souls, was their mission to spread the knowledge of the true faith among millions of the Yellow race in that inexpressibly strange Empire which now is in a condition of the most complete anarchy and uproar.

Among these gentle Sisters of Charity, who had forsaken home and fatherland for the sake of Jesus Crucified, were French, Belgian, and Italian, but only one of Irish nationality, bearing the fine old name of

* This work was first published at the end of the nineteenth century. The massacre of Tien-tsin took place in 1870.

7

O'Sullivan. Her short history, her life in China, and her martyrdom will be of interest to Irish readers, who are specially ready to admire the apostolic labours of their own missionaries—men and women who have inherited the zeal for souls that urged so many of our ancient monks to leave their beloved land to preach the Gospel to nations " sitting in darkness."

Alice O'Sullivan, known in the religious life as " Sœur Louise," was born in 1836, at Clonmel, a picturesque town on the River Suir, situated opposite some pretty hills sloping down to the stream, which half a mile further flows through one of the most fertile and lovely valleys of Tipperary. In this thriving and prosperous town, then the centre of a great trade in corn and other agricultural produce, Alice's parents had settled* not very long before the birth of their little girl, who, being very fragile, was baptised almost immediately. Mrs. O'Sullivan dying while Alice was a mere baby, the child was left very much to the care of a devoted nurse, who, like many other women of her class, rather spoiled her little charge, and permitted her much more liberty than a mother would have done. Alice's brothers, all older than herself, naturally made a great deal of the little sister who was always eager to join

* They had originally belonged to Newry, in the Co. Armagh.

in their games. She learned to read at a
very early period, and she had a great
love of reading, which she was allowed to
indulge as she pleased. But as the books,
though much beyond her age, were fortunately not bad, they did not do her any
great harm beyond exciting her lively
southern imagination. Thanks, no doubt,
to the influence of the very simple-minded
if injudicious old nurse, Alice was, even as
a very young child, inclined to piety, and
she was always exceedingly fond of the poor.

In St. Mary's Presentation Convent,
Irishtown, Clonmel, where she received
her girlhood education, secular and religious, she was a great favourite with the
nuns, some of whom still survive, and
speak of her with great affection. Indeed,
the whole community feel justly proud of
this, that their convent has been instru-
mental in sending religious to all parts of
the world. One branch has taken no fewer
than thirty-six nuns from this foundation.
When about ten years old this now im-
mortalised pupil of theirs showed great
piety and desire to enter religion. Going
to the Convent of the Sisters of Charity
which had then recently been established
in SS. Peter and Paul's parish, she gravely
asked to become a sister!

At a later date it was decided that she
should become a Sister of Charity, but not
of the Irish Congregation. Her brother

had become a Vincentian missionary, and it
was, no doubt, this circumstance that led to
the choice, after prayer for the light to know
God's holy will, of the Congregation of the
Sisters of Charity of St. Vincent de Paul.
A daughter of St. Vincent she would
become, and it was with a view to this,
in order that her education might be further advanced, that her father determined
to entrust her to the Dominican nuns at
Kingstown, near Dublin, where her time
passed happily under the care of the kind
Sisters. Alice's open and simple disposition
and her great piety, we are informed, so
impressed her mistresses that they would
have gladly admitted her into their community had she desired it. The present
Prioress of the Convent, who knew Alice
very intimately, and had the deepest
respect and affection for her, has been
asked to give her recollections of the appearance and character of her schoolfellow.
She very kindly replied that Alice was
rather older than most of her companions,
was dark in complexion, not particularly
handsome, but yet attractive, with a strong
sense of humour, which was combined with
a mature common sense and the truest
piety. On this point all who knew the
future martyr speak strongly.

It was not necessary for her to stay very
long at Kingstown, and then came the
parting. Courageously, in the year 1856,

she bade farewell to her father and her home on the pleasant banks of the Suir, where never again would she roam through the green fields, or climb the hills, or feel the soft Irish "rain-washed" breezes blowing on her brow. The kindly smiles and affectionate "God save you" that come so readily from our humble Irish country people she would no more see or hear from those who had known and loved her from her infancy ; the church where she knelt as a little child she would never enter again, nor the streets of the old Irish town.

Yet she never faltered, but departed to follow the call to a more perfect life—a life of obedience, of toil, of self-abnegation, of prayer, and union with God, in the modest and coarse greyish-blue habit and the white " cornette " of a Sister of Charity. Across two seas went Alice to the house of the Sisters at Amiens, that quiet town in Picardy, which Ruskin has called the Venice of Northern France.

Alice passed some time as a postulant in this convent, learning all the ways and customs of the new life she desired to embrace. No doubt she visited the stately mediæval Gothic cathedral, which in size is exceeded only by St. Peter's at Rome, St. Sophia's at Constantinople, and the vast German cathedral of Cologne. Very probably Alice also admired the fine statue of Our Lord on the pillar of the magnificent central

porch, which the townspeople, from the
time it was placed there, have lovingly
called their own " beau Christ d'Amiens ";
and we may be very certain she prayed
fervently before the Altar of the Blessed
Sacrament for the grace of perseverance
in her religious career.

Then Alice travelled on to the mother-
house in the Rue de Bac at Paris, where
she was to receive the habit of the Congregation and to make her novitiate. As
soon as her vows were made Alice, now
Sister Louise, was sent first to Boulogne
and then to Drogheda. Here she spent five
years among the poor of the old town, who
were very numerous and destitute. Indeed
Sister Louise often regretted she could not
alleviate the distress she so often saw as
she went on her errands of charity through
the narrow lanes and winding stairways that
connect the upper streets with the lower
ones on the banks of the historic Boyne.
Sister Louise, or as, perhaps, we had better
continue to call her, Alice O'Sullivan, passed
also some time at Hereford, where the
mission was full of struggle and hardships.
Long ago when she was still a gay school-
girl about sixteen years old, she said to a
very dear friend one day : " Later on you
will see I shall go to China, and there die
a martyr "—words which were destined to
be fully realised.

CHAPTER II

THE CALL TO CHINA

ALICE was chosen by Providence for a high destiny—no less than the glory of shedding her blood for Christ in China. We shall have to trace her career in the country, and first we must point out how the call came to devote her life to the far-off mission of Cathay. God has different methods of drawing souls—to some He gives the sweet consolation of Divine Love here, for others He reserves it for a future life. Alice was led by the hard way of the cross, by the way of suffering and obedience. It never entered her head to request Superiors to send her to the Far East. She knew very little about it—but when the call of obedience came, it found her ready.

When she had entered the Vincentian Congregation, she had frequently, we are told, expressed to her Superiors her willingness to be employed on any distant mission they might select for her. It was no light sacrifice she thus made, for she dearly loved her own people and her native land, and would have rejoiced to live and die in Ireland, working for its sick and its poor. But her generous offer was not

13

forgotten, and when it was decided that
Sisters of Charity were to take charge of a
hospital at Shanghai, Alice O'Sullivan
was named among the band of foreign
Sisters who were going to set out on the
long journey to China.

On their arrival at Shanghai, in the year
1863, the Sisters met with a great trial
in finding that not only was there no pro-
perly equipped house for them, but that
the members of the Hospital Committee had
changed their minds and did not wish
even for their services, being quite put
out by the appearance of the Sisters at
Shanghai. Being Protestants, they could
not understand the wants of the nuns, and
indeed, they made, as we are told, "every
difficulty" about having them in the
hospital. The Sisters had to reside in a
wretched lodging, with hardly anything
in the way of furniture or food. Sister
Alice, being the only one who could speak
English, became interpreter between her
French Superioress and the gentlemen of
the Committee. It was a difficult position,
necessitating much tact and prudence,
but so well did Sister Alice fulfil her task
that in a short time the Englishmen who
had been most opposed to the employment of the Sisters became most sincere
and influential friends and protectors of
the humble daughters of St. Vincent de
Paul. The Superioress, who often expected

a refusal, was surprised to see how easily her requests were granted, and expressed her astonishment to Sister O'Sullivan, who replied gently : " It is the Blessed Virgin and my guardian angel who have done it all ; before I came I confided this affair to them, and it is they who have brought it to a successful issue."

In the hospital, where the Sisters were soon hard at work, Sister Alice was invaluable as an attendant upon Irish, English, and American sailors and soldiers, who could not understand her French or Belgian companions. In a letter, written to her Lazarist brother, Alice tells him how, on St. Patrick's Day, 1867, thirty Irish soldiers came to pay her a visit and to present her with five pounds for the poor out of their meagre pay. In the Presentation Convent, Clonmel, mentioned above, there is shown a very handsome statue of St. Joseph, erected by the devotion of some soldiers who had been quartered in the town, and one of whose number had been kindly treated at the Convent. They also accompanied Sister Alice to say the Rosary together in the chapel, and the much edified Reverend Mother gave a number of pictures representing the Holy Father, which greatly pleased the Irish soldiers, whose sincere piety and charity was much appreciated by the good Sisters.

In the hospital Sister O'Sullivan's charm

of manner and heartfelt kindness had
immense influence over the sick, one of
whom, a Scotch Presbyterian Freemason,
wrote to the Catholic Archbishop of Dublin
after the massacre that " amongst those
saints was my kind-hearted nurse, Sister
Louise, who was at my bedside day and
night, cheering my drooping spirits broken
down with sickness and pain. Often she
told me how delighted she was, although
far away from old Ireland, to have the
privilege of conversing in her native tongue
with a Scotchman. I will not dwell longer
on the characteristics of this ministering
angel, who is now with her Redeemer." As
one of her Superiors wrote, she was at once
simple and engaging, and it was impossible
to live with her without loving her.

Yet this serene and amiable friendliness,
always shown to everyone by Sister Alice,
was most meritorious as far as the Chinese
were concerned, whose dispositions and
customs excited her greatest repugnance,
amounting to antipathy. To have made the
sacrifice to go on this arduous mission, and
to find that she could not sympathise with
nor comprehend the people for whom she
had given up all that was dearest to her,
must have indeed been a dreadful trial ; but
she sought for strength and endurance
from Our Lord, who is never " displeased
when we feel a repugnance to a sacrifice
that He asks from us."

We shall, therefore, give not scandal but edification by noting that this warm-hearted young Irish Sister of Charity implies in one of her letters that God had not rewarded her good-will with much sensible consolation. "I am now, thank God," she writes, "quite at peace, only that now and then I feel a little lonely, but happy in having nothing to trouble my conscience, and with great trust in God, Who has taken such care of me up to this time." * This repugnance felt by Sister Alice has been often felt by many a poor missionary striving with all his might against the innumerable evils in a district often larger than many a European diocese, surrounded by millions of the Yellow race enslaved by the grossest superstition. One French priest remarked once: "Talk to the Chinese of religion, of a God, of heaven or hell, and they yawn ; speak to them of business, and they are all attention. If ever you hear of a Chinaman who is not a thief or a liar, do not believe it ; they are thieves and liars every one."† Yet this Catholic missionary still continued with unflinching devotion to convert his un-compromising people, just as Sister Alice, often yearning for her far-distant island

---

* *Irish Monthly*, vol. v.
† We do not, of course, quote this saying as being just, but merely to show what the poor French priest thought about the Chinese.

home with its kindly Catholic people, strove to devote herself to her Apostolic work among the peculiar and often most unattractive people of the Celestial Empire.

The Sisters were destined to do a great work in the Shanghai hospital. It was for many years under their charge till recently they surrendered it voluntarily to another Congregation. Their reason for doing this was that they desired to work exclusively for the native Chinese ; whereas the General Hospital at Shanghai was resorted to by European patients only. It is, however, an undoubted fact that during the earlier period the possession of the hospital had brought them into contact with large numbers of influential persons, especially belonging to the Military and Naval services of Great Britain and other European Powers, and that not merely was the position of the nuns thereby immensely strengthened, but in many ways the Catholic cause benefited by the protection which officers and others felt bound to provide in return for the valuable services the Vincentian Sisters had rendered to themselves or others. Thus many regretted that the Sisters had to relinquish the work : no doubt they felt that in changed circumstances their presence in the hospital had become less necessary.

CHAPTER III

THE HOLY CHILDHOOD AT PEKIN

IN the year 1867, Sister Alice O'Sullivan was stationed at Pekin, travelling thither with Mother Azais, who was the Visitor of the Houses of the Sisters of Charity in "Far Cathay." They, of course, went by sea from Shanghai to Tien-tsin, the great seaport of Northern China, which is connected by the winding river Pei-ho with the Yellow Sea. The house boats take from two to three days sailing towards Pekin, between the flat banks of an apparently ugly country, composed of alluvial mud, which is frequently inundated, and on which are to be seen numbers of villages, some large and some small, but all built of repulsive looking mud, though there are few signs of poverty, the district being extremely fertile. Of course the railway between Tien-tsin and Pekin, lately destroyed by the Boxers, did not exist at that period, so that the two Sisters of Charity proceeded by the river as far as they could, and then they traversed the short distance to Pekin that still intervened in one of those dreadful Pekin carts which are constantly used in this part of China.

19

These vehicles are quite devoid of springs, which could never resist the strain of the atrocious apologies for roads in this part of the world, and they are somewhat in the shape of a low trolley with a blue hood, drawn by sturdy mules or ponies. The misery of travelling in such a cart, though often enough described, must be experienced in order to realise the horrible sensation it produces on those who are compelled to drive in it.

Clouds of dust resembling ashes, according to a Jesuit missionary, are to be met at every turn in the noisy streets of the Chinese capital, of which the following brilliant description may interest my readers : " There are three Pekins : exterior Pekin, as it is seen from the city walls a delicious wilderness of green trees, in the depths of which dust and nastiness are submerged, and from whose leafy surface rise the curled roofs of yellow-tiled palaces, temples, pagodas, or distant towers; interior Pekin, of the streets, tumultuous, kaleidoscopic, pestilential, shrill ; and the innermost Pekin, or the mysterious, hidden behind the pink and yellow walls that conceal from alien eyes the penetralia both of secular and spiritual adoration. The first of these is the only aspect in which charm is unshattered by jarring associations, although when we descend into it we wonder where the shade and the verdure

have gone to, so completely do they seem
to have disappeared."

Then comes an account by the same
writer, of one street, which will serve as
a description of all the others, and enable
the reader to form an accurate mental
picture of the daily life of Chinamen in
Pekin. "In a main street, whose great
breadth is successfully concealed by two
lines of booths that have sprung up in the
kind of ditch that extends on either side
of the elevated central roadway, through
the dust, we may discern a long vista, the
parallel walls of which present a line of
fantastic poles, gilded signboards, carved
woodwork, and waving streamers and
lanterns—the insignia and advertisements
of the shops that open below. Down this
avenue jostles and streams a perpetual
crowd of blue-clad, long-queued (pig-tailed),
close-shaven, brazen-lunged men; Chinese
women, hobbling feebly on their mutilated
stumps, thickly-rouged Tartar wives, a
sparsely-bearded mandarin seen nodding
behind his saucer-like spectacles in a
screened sedan; long strings of splendid
two-humped camels, parading a magnificent winter coat, and blinking a supercilious
eye, as they stalk along to the heavy
cadence of the leader's bell, laden with
sacks of lime or coal from the hills; Mon-
golians in shaggy caps bestriding still
shaggier ponies; half-naked coolies wheel-

ing casks of oil, or buckets of manure, on
creeking barrows; boys perched on the
tails of minute donkeys; ramshackle
wagons, drawn by mixed teams of mules,
asses, ponies, and oxen; abominable and
hairy black pigs running in and out of the
animals' legs; good-looking, but cowardly
dogs that bark, and, above all, the crash
and roar of the ubiquitous Pekin cart,
thundering with studded wheels over stone
bridges, and crashing into the deep ruts, and
drawn by the most majestic mules in Asia,
cruelly bitted with a wire across their gums.
This is the panorama of the central aisle.

" In the side aisles or alleys, all the more
stationary purveyors of the amusements
and necessities of life are jammed up
together; barbers shaving without soap
their stolid customers; dentists and chiro-
pedists proclaiming their extraordinary
skill; auctioneers proclaiming the glories
of second-hand blouses and pantaloons;
cobblers punching the thick soles of the
native shoe; gamblers playing dominoes
or backing against all comers a well-
nurtured fighting cricket; pedlars and
hucksters, curio-dealers offering jade snuff-
boxes or porcelain bowls; vendors of the
opium pipe, charm sellers, and quacks
with trays of strange powders and nauseat-
ing drugs; acrobats performing feats of
agility; story-tellers enchanting an open-
mouthed crowd; musicians tweaking a

single-stringed guitar ; country folk vend-
ing immense white cabbages or ruddy red
persimmons ; soldiers with bows and
arrows ; coolies drawing water from im-
memorial wells ; and men and boys of every
age carrying birds in cages or a singing
chaffinch attached by a string to a stick.
A more than ordinary shouting will herald
the approach of a bridal procession, in
which the bride, locked into an embroidered
red palanquin, follows after a train of boys
bearing lanterns and men blowing trumpets
and tapping drums ; or of a funeral cortège,
in which the corpse, preceded by umbrellas
and tablets, rests upon a gigantic red bier,
with difficulty borne upon the shoulders of
several scores of men.

" In curious contrast with the roar of this
many-tongued crowd, a melodious whirring
sings in the air, and is produced by whistles
attached to the tails of domestic pigeons."*

Through such scenes and sounds did
Sister Alice O'Sullivan and Mother Azais
in their Pekin cart pass, on their way to the
convent, and in a very short time Sister
Alice was busily employed in the infant
school and the orphanage, which play a
most important part in the great work of
the Holy Childhood carried out in our
Chinese missions.

This Society, for the redemption of pagan
children, was established among European

* *Problems of the Far East,* Lord Curzon of Kedleston.

children during the pontificate of Pius IX.,
towards the middle of the nineteenth
century, and its special work, entrusted
to the Sisters of Charity in China, was the
support and education of baby girls, who
are so frequently killed or abandoned by
their inhuman mothers; many of whom
have the firm conviction that infants are
born without souls, which only develop at
a more advanced period of existence; consequently there can be no harm in getting
rid of such superfluous mouths as those of
little girls, who are numerous enough
everywhere.

Mr. Morrison, in his charming book,
An Australian in China, says that it is
very customary for infant girls, if they be
not destroyed, to be sold into slavery, and
carried in baskets, like poultry, to the
capital to be sold for wives. The fate of
such children, until they are old enough to
be married, is extremely sad. They are
beaten and shamefully ill-treated by their
future mothers-in-law, some of whom, if
the wretched little slave be very sickly or
maimed by ill-usage, will think nothing of
turning the poor child out to die like a dog
in the street. Should, however, the child
grow up strong and well, she is married,
and in the twinkle of an eye all is changed,
and she meets with the greatest deference
and attention. But, alas for Chinese human nature! when this matron, who has

SISTER OF CHARITY WITH CATHOLIC ORPHAN.

had such a terrible childhood, is able to
purchase in her turn a little slave, quite
unmindful of her past experience, she is
just as hard and cruel as was her mother-
in-law before her.   And so it goes on, this
sad abuse, ever repeating itself in the
families of pagan Chinese, and hence the
immense importance of the work of the
Holy Childhood, supporting annually an
immense number of persons, and main-
tained by the Sisters of Charity.

In 1862 Monseigneur Mouly took out from
France for Pekin and Tien-tsin fourteen
Sisters of Charity, who in both places at
once set about the establishment of the Holy
Childhood, baptising dying babies, collect-
ing those who were abandoned in the streets,
putting them out at nurse, then receiving
them into the orphanage at a suitable age.
These poor Chinese children, under the care
of the excellent Sisters, grew up pious and
worthy Catholic girls, many of whom
married, and founded good Catholic families, while others either became school-
mistresses of the Holy Childhood schools,
Virgins of Purgatory, or Josephines, which
is another Chinese religious congregation,
and even Sisters of Charity. Down to
the present day has this noble work of the
Holy Childhood effected incalculable good
in China ; and is, consequently, specially
hated by the demons whose power is still
very great in the Celestial Empire.

CHAPTER IV

THE GREAT RENUNCIATION

WE now come to a very curious and interesting episode in Alice's history. Or rather, it is the true turning point in that history, the actual martyrdom of the good Irish nun being in reality only a sequel to the choice which she then made under extraordinary circumstances. There are occasions in our own lives or in those of others which seem to bring before us, almost in a tangible way, the presence of the supernatural ; and the incident we are about to relate appears to be a very marked occurrence of the same sort.

Sister Alice now felt that she was really in China, coming in contact with so many natives in the course of her labours, and she wrote that Our Lord gave her great consolation " because we receive almost every day little babies, and I hold them for the Sacrament of Baptism." But though she did her best to overcome her great disgust of China, and its really trying and peculiar customs, yet she could not become used to the Chinese. Finally, in the year 1870, after many a struggle with herself, she determined to write to Père Etienne,

26

the Superior-General of the Lazarists and
Sisters of Charity, and to tell him of her
failure to acclimatise herself in her Eastern
surroundings. He answered her by au-
thorising her to return to France with the
Sister Visitor, who was on the point of
making this voyage. This letter caused her
intense pleasure. To see once more the
civilisation of Europe, to escape her daily
struggle with her repugnance for the
Chinese, to make this voyage with Sister
Azais—all this enchanted her ; and they
started together for the seaport of Tien-tsin
on their way home from Pekin.

A Catholic missionary described Tien-tsin
as being like the surrounding country, grey
and dusty ; and that there was enormous
traffic in the streets, which were crowded
with people, great wheelbarrows, jinrick-
shas, and the heavy carts used everywhere
in North China. The eating-houses and
tea-shops are generally full of boisterous
customers. The people are of a thrifty,
hard-working race, strong-limbed and in-
domitable, but they have always, especially
at Tien-tsin, borne an extremely bad
reputation. Ungracious, arrogant, over-
bearing, and intensely conceited, they are
most quarrelsome amongst themselves,
"continually fighting in the most violent
way, pulling the hair and fracturing the
limbs of their adversaries, and very often
leaving them half dead." Contempt

would be a mild term to express the hatred
and scorn they feel for the " devils from
the west," at whom they did not hesitate
to spit, or to call them by the most oppro-
brious epithets, in which the Chinese
language is remarkably rich. Absorbed as
these people were in the interests of this
world, and full of intolerable prejudices,
the missionaries working among them in
those early days, between 1862 and 1870,
had indeed need of patience and trust in
God, Who alone could assist them in their
newly-established   and   most   difficult
mission.

Sister O'Sullivan, with Mother Azais,
stopped at Tien-tsin, and went to the
Convent of the Sisters of Charity, known
as the " Jen-tse-t'ang," and established
since 1862. Here were two orphanages
for boys and girls, a dispensary, and a
hospital for Europeans which had just been
founded. The Sisters, who were all too
few in number for their numerous works of
mercy, had been making a Novena that
their community should be increased by
some English-speaking Sister, whose services were indispensable in an hospital
frequented by many British and American
subjects connected with the vast shipping
trade of the port.

Consequently, on the arrival of Sister
O'Sullivan, they at once begged her to
remain with them and undertake this im-

portant post in the hospital. Poor Sister Alice could scarcely believe her ears. Was she really to forego the chance allowed her by her Superiors of returning to Europe to be once more among her own people, to hear again the language of her childhood, to look into the kindly eyes of dearly-loved friends and relations, so widely different in every single thought and habit from the repugnant Chinese, these cold-hearted, deceitful, and often cruel people, of whom, with all the good-will in the world, she had never been able to conquer her instinctive aversion.

Our readers may remark that Sisters of any religious Order are supposed to be quite indifferent as to what part of the world they may be sent to ; but it is often forgotten that although these pious, unselfish women have made the sacrifice of kindred, home, and country, to "follow the Lamb," their feelings and their affections are by no means deadened, and many is the bitter struggle which, through God's holy grace, and earnest prayer, is nobly overcome, by souls wrung and almost crushed under the anguish of the trial. Now had come to the poor little Irish Sister the bitterest hour of her existence. Her warm, southern nature rose vehemently against the suggestion of the companions whom she thought almost cruel in even wishing to detain her. Our Irish people

are, as a rule, exceedingly attached to their
families and their homes, but the inhabitants of our great southern province are
particularly noted for this love of kindred
and country.   With them it often amounts
to a passion.   Sister O'Sullivan was thoroughly Irish, and no one, excepting her
own country people, could realise the over-
whelming joy she felt at the idea of going
back, were it only for a short time.   She
could return to China later with a better
spirit for the work ; she could during her
absence interest friends who would help
on the great Chinese Mission.

Her permission to go home had been
granted by Père Etienne, and surely, as
Superior-General, he would never have
granted it did he think it would injure her
soul.   As one of the Sisters wrote later,
it was easy to see how the mere idea that she
could be expected to renounce her journey
aroused her intense excitement and indig-
nation.   Mother Azais having expressed
a wish to visit the new Catholic church
just erected at Tien-tsin by the Lazarist
missionary, M. Chevrier, and dedicated by
him to Our Lady of Victories, a carriage
was procured, and some of the Sisters
joined her and Sister O'Sullivan on the
little pilgrimage.

During the drive the question was again
mooted about Sister Alice remaining at
Tien-tsin, and she really became quite

angry at the persistency of the Sisters.
They all entered the church, and after their
devotions the Missionary Father asked them
to come and look at the exterior of the
edifice he had erected with so much zeal
and care. Sister O'Sullivan, however, remained behind. There she knelt before
the silent tabernacle in the quiet church,
her heart rent with conflicting feelings.
Surely God having accepted the sacrifice
of her whole existence did not wish that
she should remain in China. He must see
how very lonely she was, not even one Irish
Sister or priest or friend in the whole of
the strange Chinese town to whom she
could turn for counsel—only these foreigners,
who kind and good though they were, could
not understand her utter loneliness, or
what the giving up of the journey meant to
her.

It must have been a great agony for
the poor Sister, kneeling before the Blessed
Sacrament, struggling whether to admit the
Divine Will that she should make this
supreme renunciation of her cherished
wish. We are told by Father Faber that
"holiness of the highest kind is distinguished by the quickness and fineness of
its ear in detecting inspiration, and by its
promptitude and docility in following
them." Now, Sister O'Sullivan was an
extremely holy soul, and when she recognised the voice of Jesus gently calling her

to accept this cross and follow Him, all
hesitation, all doubts, all opposition instantly ceased, and the renunciation (a
very real mental martyrdom to the little
Sister), was simply made : " Not my will,
but Thine, O Lord."

It has been thought that our Blessed
Lady came to her in those moments of
agonizing pain and encouraged her to hear
and obey unreservedly the call to duty and
self-sacrifice from the Holy Spirit, whom
as Our Lord Himself has said, " breatheth
where He will." Into these few minutes
had been compressed the combat and the
glorious victory over human nature. When
the other Sisters came to fetch the Irish
nun they were electrified to hear her say,
" I am not going home, oh, I will not go."
" What in the world has happened, dear
Sister ? " they exclaimed. She answered :
" If I were to tell you, you would not believe
me." She hastened to find Sister Azais,
and told her that she placed herself at her
disposal to remain in China if she thought
it was God's will. Sister Azais said to her
at the moment of departure : " Good-bye
till we meet again." Sister O'Sullivan
answered : " We shall never meet again
in this world. You will return, but we
shall all be gone."

Whatever had happened, a miracle of
grace had been worked in the soul of Sister
Alice through the intermediary of Our

Lady of Victories. She went into the church full of trouble, and she came out of it entirely changed. She herself gave us this assurance and affirmed the intervention of Our Lady in the following letter, written to the Father-General, M. Etienne :—

TIEN-TSIN, *May 4th*, 1870.

VERY REV. FATHER,—Your blessing I beg of you. I follow the inspiration which urges me to write to you, but I do not like to take up your time which is so precious, Very Rev. Father, especially in these days when all the children of St. Vincent come from the different quarters of the globe to wish you joy, both by voice and by letter. How happy I am to be reckoned among the members of your family, although the humblest and last of your dear daughters, but not the least grateful ! I only ask for a few moments of time, most honoured Father, to express to you myself the great gratitude which I feel for the permission which you had granted me to return to France with our good and reverend Mother Azais. Thanks, to God and to Our Lady of Victories, who is as powerful at Tien-tsin as at Paris, my heart, which had suffered from illusions for so long a time, has been entirely changed, and to-day I fully understand why it will be more perfect for me to remain till death in this poor country.

Besides, Very Rev. Father, I reckon on
the Blessed Virgin to give me the grace of
perseverance in this resolution, for it was
she herself who said to me: 'Remain
for the rest of your life with these
people.' I feel sure that it is, thanks to
your fervent prayers, that my eyes have
been opened to see the will of God regarding my future. Again and again, therefore,
do I thank you for your charity towards
your poor little Irish child. I cannot
express to you how much I owe you, and
it is at the feet of Our Lady of Victories
that I pray with all my heart for you and
for the community. Pray send us back
our good Mother Azais as soon as you can.
I have the honour to be, in the love of Our
Lord and His Immaculate Mother,

Your respectful and obedient daughter,

SISTER LOUISE (ALICE) O'SULLIVAN.

Having once made up her mind to
remain, Sister O'Sullivan set to work with
renewed ardour ; it seemed as if a secret
presentiment of the end of her double exile
being near at hand pressed her to labour
more urgently so as to make an ample
harvest of merit. She, however, ignored
this altogether, and while her virtue
edified all around her, and heaven was
preparing her crown, she was always
humbling herself at the fact that her com-

panions served the Chinese with pleasure,
while she had to do constant violence to
herself to overcome her antipathy, which
she attributed to her want of generosity.
In the last letter written by her Superior,
Sister Marquet, to the community we read :
" We are very happy to have Sister O'Sullivan. Our Lady of Victories has not done
her work by halves ! I do not think our
dear little Sister has any thought now of
leaving China. She is a devoted worker,
and does all that is in her power to supply
the place of any of the Sisters who may
be ill or convalescent, and unable to fulfil
the duties of their office."

But in reality, though she did not know
it, the sacrifice she had made was to prepare
her for a greater one—the greatest grace
that perhaps God could give her—that of
actually shedding her blood in testimony of
the truth of Jesus Christ, and His religion.
It has been remarked that the grace of
martyrdom, like all sovereign graces, has to
be purchased by correspondence with other
and smaller ones. This law, whether uni-
versal or not, was certainly verified in the
case of the martyr of Clonmel. But we
will proceed with her simple story.

Besides the struggles of which we have
spoken, Sister O'Sullivan often suffered
from desolation of spirit, in proportion to
the tender piety she felt towards God.
But her lively faith enabled her to bear

even this desolation. She continued to
draw nearer God with an equal confidence,
as to a loving father, feeling as sure of His
tenderness when He sent her suffering as
when He deigned to console her. Was she
in any trouble ? Did she desire any
special grace ? She went to throw herself
at Our Lord's feet with an instinctive conviction that her prayer would be granted.
This simple faith was evidently very
pleasing to Him, for she almost invariably
obtained what she wished. Holy Communion and Jesus in the Blessed Sacrament
was the furnace whence Sister O'Sullivan
drew all her fervour. When near the
tabernacle of the Divinity she was con-
soled for everything, and hence flowed her
devotion to the poor, a devotion which cannot be expressed in words.

April and the sweet month of May passed
by in the Jen-tse-t'ang, where Sister O'Sullivan and her companions carried out their
works of mercy with their usual zeal and
devotion among the Chinese. This mission
of the Sisters of Charity at Tien-tsin was
one of the most remarkable foundations
of their Congregation. So curious and
extraordinary were the incidents connected
with it that we must give a description of
it to our readers. At first the Sisters had
been left in a very small house which was
almost bare of even the most needful furniture. Five chairs and two huge Chinese

saucepans seem to have been their chief possessions, and to add to the discomfort their luggage did not arrive with them but a long time afterwards. At first there was not a single child or sick person, and "the Sisters found themselves in a kind of desert in the midst of these people."

However, nothing daunted, the Sisters by degrees opened an orphanage, a dispensary, and a hospital. The cholera breaking out, the Bishop brought a workman attacked by the epidemic to the Sisters who succeeded in saving his life. On his recovery he very naturally told all his friends of his wonderful cure, and in a very short time the dispensary was crowded with patients seeking relief. "Here," writes a Sister," we had another great difficulty ; our pharmacy had not arrived, and we had none of the necessary medicines. All we could do was to pray to Our Lord to bless and make efficacious the little things we had at our disposal. In our little travelling medicine case we had two bottles of Chartreuse, which Our Lord really multiplied ; also a case of mustard. We were delighted to see these poor fellows every day in rows in our courtyard, each with two little glasses in their hands, in one of which we poured a little Chartreuse, and in the other camphorated spirits for frictions ; while we added a little packet of mustard for poultices."

CHAPTER V

WORKS OF MERCY AT TIEN-TSIN

So here we find Sister Alice staying to devote herself at a critical period to works of mercy in that very town of Tien-tsin where she was soon to win her glorious crown of martyrdom.

Writing to the Superior-General at Paris the Sister Visitor observed that it was extraordinary, six days after the arrival of the Sisters, to witness, every day, crowds of people at their doors begging the Sisters to come and visit their sick who were victims of the Asiatic cholera. She goes on to say : "The care and skill given by our Sisters to the sick were manifestly blessed by God ; a good number recovered ; and the consequence was that in a very short time we gained such a reputation that it was impossible to check the crowd coming to us for remedies against this terrible malady. I am obliged to restrain the zeal of our Sisters, who are so few, lest they should sink from fatigue. They are now only allowed to go out in our own quarter. Only a few minutes ago I went with Sister Dutrouilh to see the son of our butcher. If you but knew with what respect they received us—you could not really have an idea of it. I fancy your saying: 'But what about the language?' My dear Father, it is indeed a reason to feel that heaven is helping us; we take a Chinese Christian girl, who understands us a little, and who acts as our interpreter. And then what remedies have we? A little mustard powder, tea, oil, rice water. May we not really declare that our good God works with us?"

When Father Etienne received this letter, in a conference he was then giving, December 8th, 1862, he exclaimed: "Our Sisters have gone to unfurl the flag of charity in the capital of that vast empire, so long the prey of the powers of evil. They find themselves, on landing at Tientsin, in the midst of a violent outbreak of cholera. This was the harvest of good work which they hastened to reap; they found a heap of dying children whom they hastened to baptise and send to heaven, and many others who recovered, thanks to their care. But the charity of Jesus Christ has begun to spread, through them, His divine light and His genial warmth over these immense countries, darkened and frozen by the vices of infidelity and paganism. They have, in fact, undertaken the conquest of this multitude sitting in the shadow of death. A mission which thus begins its work has a magnificent destiny before it."

This destiny, indeed, was to be far more sublime than he knew, for the martyr's crown was eventually to be God's own high reward to these zealous daughters of St. Vincent de Paul.

But in the midst of their joy came the cross in the shape of Sister Pavillon's sudden attack of the epidemic. Sister Azais told the Superior-General, however, that " our prayers have been heard ; after greatest anxiety, this good Sister has been declared out of danger, She begs me to tell you that she was not good enough. I told her that she must work for ten years more before she dies ! You see that Our Lord loves us, as He allows us to share His cross. Help us to thank Him.

" Among the persons who came to the dispensary was a woman, the daughter and the widow of a mandarin, who attracted our attention. During her husband's last illness, she promised the devil, of whom she was a very fervent worshipper, to give him her daughter, if only he would save her husband's life. But the husband died, and naturally she thought no more of her vow. Then the devil began to torment her and her daughter every night, and beat them so cruelly that the girl, who was only nine years old, became deformed. As the poor woman was a simple and straightforward person, she did everything she could to get rid of this terrible

though invisible enemy, and at last she
heard an interior voice saying to her that
some Europeans who were coming would
deliver her. No sooner did the Sisters
arrive, than she felt convinced that they
were the people who were to help her, and
she came every day to the dispensary,
bringing her poor daughter with her, whose
extreme weakness and thinness made us
think that her malady was incurable, as
we knew nothing of the circumstances."

After giving details of the exor-
cisms employed, the Sister added : " The
more the poor woman advanced in her
religious instruction the more these terrible
crises diminished. It was touching to see
her, the moment she was left in peace,
make the sign of the cross and remain for
hours on her knees in the chapel, repeating,
' I believe in God, I love God.' She would
always find sweetness and peace in these
words, so powerful and mysterious is the
link which exists between the Heart of
Our Lord and that of His creature. Her
child was the first who was exorcised, and
one of the Sisters having sewn a picture
of the Immaculate Conception on the
breast and back of the child's dress, since
that day the devil dare not take possession
of one placed under the protection of Mary.
At last the holy Bishop succeeded with the
mother, and the demon was conquered.
After their baptism the mother and

daughter, who had taken the names of
Magdalen and Cecilia, implored to remain
with the Sisters, too happy to be employed
in the most humble occupations about the
house.

The mother gave her daughter to the
work of the Holy Infancy, and devoted
herself completely to the Sisters' service.
This decision caused a violent persecution
of both from their family, some powerful
members of whom treated them with the
greatest indignity. The affair was at last
brought by the French Consul before the
Chinese tribunals ; and the mandarins gave
judgment in favour of the neophytes. The
grandfather had determined to bring about
the death of his granddaughter. He was
at Tien-tsin at the moment of the massacres, and we shall see Cecilia Ho refusing
every temptation to return to her family,
so as not to run the risk of losing her faith.
This poor girl was thoroughly worthy of
the Sisters' care and instruction, and even
wished earnestly to share in their
martyrdom.

So grateful were the Chinese for the
assistance of the Sisters during the course
of the cholera epidemic, that, as we are
informed " it was really marvellous to see
the proud city of Tien-tsin giving, so soon
after their arrival, the freedom of the city
to three humble servants of the poor."
The French Minister at Peking sent the

Sisters three cases of wine from Bordeaux ;
the consul of Tien-tsin a large chest of
tea, telling them to come to him in every
difficulty and trouble. He came to pay
them a visit, saw the house, and took a
most lively interest in their establishment,
only regretting that the Sisters were not
more numerous.

When Sister Alice O'Sullivan heroically
gave up her journey home to remain at the
Tien-tsin Mission, there were 200 orphans
in the Jen-tse-t'ang and 200 out at nurse,
2,007 dying children had been baptised,
48,000 sick cared for at the dispensary,
56,700 portions of soup and food given to
the starving poor, 50 adults baptised before
their deaths, and three additions were made
to the hospital, consisting of two large
halls for Chinese patients and one for
Europeans. Moreover, Brother Marty, the
architect of the Church of Our Lady of
Victories, built a pretty chapel for the
Sisters. At first shunned by the people,
who had a lively recollection of the much-
hated European armies not long departed,
the Sisters, accompanied by a Chinese
woman, became a familiar sight as they
daily visited the poor and sick at their
own homes and in the villages surrounding
the town, where many a dying infant received the sacrament of Baptism at the
hands of the pious Sisters. On account of
the cornettes the people, even those who

liked them, never called the Sisters anything but the " white devils," but they
respected them and declared they were not
like other women.

As Chinese women at Tien-tsin never
left their houses nor were to be seen in
the streets, excepting carefully shrouded
and veiled in palanquins, it caused the
natives such intense surprise to see the
Sisters of Charity calmly going about on
their house-to-house visits, that at first
it was often asked if they were men or
women. By degrees the people grew so
accustomed to the sight of the Sisters that
they would even ask them into their houses
to visit their sick, and if a child were in-
disposed it would at once be shown to
" the white devils," who were so fond of
children.

Another apostolic work that much ap-
pealed to these zealous Sisters of Charity,
was the class of the porters working in the
town. Sister Martha wrote : " They are
almost all young men coming from various
parts of China and lodged in troops in
wretched inns, whence they are pitilessly
turned out if they develop any kind of
illness. Thrown into the street, one finds
them dying, exposed to every kind of
weather. We would have gladly taken
them in and nursed them during their sickness, but the house was so small it was
utterly impossible to find room for any

one, and especially for men. God came to
our help. Alongside of our house was a
little pagoda inhabited by two old bonzes,
who consented willingly to allow us to
hire a portion of the building which would
contain about a dozen persons. We at
once installed our sick there, and thus
began our hospital. One of the first men
admitted was a poor peasant, who was
converted and gave his young son to the
Holy Childhood. He died soon after in the
most admirable dispositions, telling his
parents how happy he was to go to heaven,
and he could not take his eyes away from
his crucifix."

The Sisters were even given permission
to visit the native foundling hospital at
Tien-tsin, for the maintenance of which
the great salt merchants contributed large
sums, and "each in turn comes to live
there for a time, and thus fulfil the office
of director." The mandarins received the
Sisters at the door on their first appearance,
showed them every ward, and gave an
order to the officials to send for the Sisters
whenever the children were very ill. Thus,
during the first year alone the Sisters were
able to baptise six hundred dying children.

CHAPTER VI

THE GATHERING STORM

Up to the time we have been considering
everything seemed to go well for the nuns.
A missionary at Tien-tsin, in October,
1863, in a letter wrote that "Our works,
both in the mission and for the establishment of the Holy Childhood, will develop
themselves by degrees, but need much
labour. But the Christians are few, and
there are thousands of souls to convert.
The people of Tien-tsin are rough and
materialistic, being chiefly sailors and
boatmen. Their morals are thoroughly
corrupt, and they have an insupportable
pride which makes them quarrel all day
long—continually fighting in the most
violent way, pulling the hair and breaking
the limbs of their adversaries, and very
often leaving them half dead. They have
a supreme contempt for all foreigners, use
the most insolent expressions towards us,
and frequently spit at us to show their
aversion. Our dear Sisters at Tien-tsin
work like apostles in spite of all the difficulties they meet with. They are Sisters
of Charity, the noblest of their sex, with
the courage of men, and all the qualities

46

of the ' valiant woman ' in Holy Scripture.
During the last year they have been able
to remove many prejudices. Their works
speak for themselves, and even the Chinese
understand that clearly. Although they
detest all Europeans, and bear with them
unwillingly, they still have confidence in
them."

A new large house belonging to a
mandarin, and formerly a barrack for
British troops, being purchased in 1864,
the Sisters were enabled to carry out their
various apostolic undertakings with much
greater success. From this period to 1867,
when Sister Alice O'Sullivan arrived at
Tien-tsin, everything seemed to be pros-
pering at the large and extensive Jen-tse-
t'ang, in spite of an epidemic of typhus
in the city, and the sudden death from
apoplexy or fever of a good Sister, who
that very morning had been engaged as
usual in the dispensary.

It was also from this year that the
great admiration and respect for the
Sisters began to diminish, as the evil
spirit, who seems to consider China as
being his own special preserve, excited
fanatical pagans to circulate many false
reports concerning the foreign missioners.
Still the majority of the people greatly
esteemed the nuns, and readily lauded
their charity and their devoted attention
to the poor, the orphans, and the sick,

and for some time nothing appeared that could cause any suspicion of danger to the mission. It was, however, the calm that precedes a storm. There had been a drought of eight months' duration, which was succeeded by one of those fearful inundations that converted the great plain into a sea. Most of the villages—which, as I have said already, were all built of mud—crumbled away, and many human beings were swept away by the floods, as well as the numerous coffins from submerged graveyards, which was particularly painful to the Chinese, who always pay much reverence to their dead. During such inundations relatives will make every effort, though often ineffectual, to save the coffins of their ancestors by fastening them to trees or posts. This particular inundation around Tien-tsin not having subsided before the winter, the plain, consequently, had become, as it were, a frozen sea.

Numbers of the country people, flooded out of their homes, had taken refuge in Tien-tsin, but no employment was to be found; starvation soon stared them in the face, with its attendant fevers and general sickness, brought on by a black paste of dry herbs, salt, and putrid fish, that constituted the food of the wretched people. The babies sent at this time to the Sisters' crèche arrived in such a condition that

CHAPEL OF CHARITY CONVENT, NING-PO.

they died like flies in spite of all attempts
to save them. Then followed an epidemic
in the orphanage, and the Sisters, over-
whelmed with work, also suffered severely
in health, while two were prostrated by
typhus, which, indeed, was raging as well
as typhoid. The sick were brought in
baskets to the hospital and dispensary,
and so crowded were the wards that they
lay about on the floors.

During the early part of 1870 a number
of fanatics, hating foreigners and their
religion, came to Tien-tsin, which was
already full enough of riff-raff and the
usual scum of a Chinese treaty port.
These gentry began their campaign against
the missioners with the usual unpleasant
secrecy in which Chinese so well know
how to conceal their nefarious plots. A
horrid pamphlet or book was circulated
about this time, entitled *Death Blow to
Corrupt Doctrines*, written in terms
analogous to the description given by the
infidel historian Gibbon in his account of
the persecutions of the early Church. So
infamous and mischievous was this work
that many protests against its circulation
were made to the Imperial Government.
Then, as is always the case in China when
the people wish to denounce something
or somebody they dislike, anonymous
placards and squibs were industriously
distributed, with the well-worn accusation

4

that the missionaries and the Sisters of
Charity were in the habit of tearing out
the eyes and hearts of Chinese children
for medicinal purposes.   An accusation of
that kind is always sure to be credited by
an ignorant Chinese mob, as their own
physicians have been known to recommend
as a cure a piece of human flesh, and a
person who will cut off a bit of his or her
own flesh to save the life of a parent is
held in the highest estimation by the
neighbours.   But this admiration is never
extended to the foreign devils, who are
accused of impiously turning Chinese eyes
and hearts into drugs.   For them nothing
can be bad enough in the way of punishment.

   As the Spring advanced and the frozen
plain melted beneath the welcome rays
of brilliant sunshine, and the earth grew
green once more, the Sisters and missionaries
began to observe a great change in the
demeanour, not only of the roughs, but
even of respectable people of Tien-tsin.
As Baron von Hubner wrote : " The good
Sisters, who used to be welcomed everywhere, only met with cold and angry looks
when they went out, and no one would be
civil or make way for them.   One evening
angry groups gathered before their house,
and it was the same next day.   The ac-
cusations were multiplied ; certain things
were asserted as facts and believed.   There

was no actual disorder yet, but a deep
dissatisfaction and menacing symptoms.
This immense Tien-tsin population trembled
like the green leaves in a forest under the
first gusts of wind which precede a storm."*

As the rabble became more and more
insulting in words and behaviour, the
Sisters at the end of May, 1870, dis-
continued their visits to the sick poor in
the town and neighbouring villages. Then
one Sunday, the porter at the Yamen, or
residence of the Chinese prefect, the
" Tao-Tai " of Tien-tsin, while the Christians were coming away from Mass, was
overheard exclaiming " This is the day,
then, when the Christians go to eat the
medicine that makes them mad "—a
scoffing allusion to the Holy Eucharist.
He was struck by an officer of the quay
and the guardian of the French Consulate
close by, who would have arrested him
had not the people forced them to release
him. Needless to say this ruffian was
among the most prominent in the massacre
now so near at hand.

The next proceeding was the violation
of the cemetery, where the heathens dug
up the coffins to see if the Sisters had been
tearing out the eyes and hearts of the
children who died in the Jen-tse-t'ang.
This naturally created deep annoyance,
and the pagans, fearing they would be

*Journey Round the World.

punished, implored the missionary, M. Chevrier, not to prosecute them. He, unfortunately, consented to overlook their conduct, which was a great mistake, as with all semi-savage races where such outrages have been perpetrated, leniency is always regarded as a sign of weakness on the part of the Europeans.

The French Consul also, who chose to listen to the lies brought him against the missionaries by such people as his pagan cook, became violently displeased with the Sisters, who, his cook informed him, bought up children, etc. It may be observed here that a few years afterwards, when the Chinese cook died, " the pagans, to their horror, saw flames coming out of his tomb and burning his coffin and his body, which they seemed to consider a visible punishment from God for his false testimony and falsehood."

This misunderstanding with Consul Fontanier, of course, considerably aggravated the anxiety of the missionaries. He seems to have been a very hot-tempered man, but was much esteemed for his other good qualities. On the subject of the increasing aversion of the pagans, nothing would alter his opinion that it had all been brought about by over-zeal on the part of the Missioners. Acting on the advice of two Englishmen, the Superioress, Sister Marquet, and Sister

O'Sullivan went to see M. Fontanier, but their representations, as well as those of the Lazarist missionary and the Russian Consul-General, failed in making any serious impression upon the unfortunate French Consul, who, although he knew there was danger, accelerated instead of averting the massacre, in which he was cruelly murdered.

The missionary, Father Chevrier, was never under any delusion as to the real state of the Chinese public mind at that period, although he saw with dismay how the hasty French Consul was, like a blind man, going headlong towards the awful precipice of a massacre of the Christians. When writing to his Superior about the threatened danger to the Tien-tsin mission, Father Chevrier said that "the Jen-tse-t'ang prays and suffers." They, too, shared in the sadness felt by their beloved Lord, when, on the eve of His Passion, he walked to the garden of Gethsemane to undergo His mysterious and indescribable agony beneath the olive trees. But we read that the Sisters pursued their apostolic labours within the Jen-tse-t'ang with the same regularity and calmness.

On account of her youthful appearance Sister Andreoni was replaced by an older Sister Clavelin in visiting the sick in their own homes. This good Sister bravely "went out, daily, affronting every insult

for the love of souls; but even she saw
with sorrow that the people of the villages,
who used to welcome them with eager-
ness, now fled at her approach as if at
a diabolical apparition."

The arrival of a violent enemy of the
foreigners, who had been mixed up in the
Tai-Ping rebellion, added fuel to the fire,
and the streets in no time were full of
dangerous placards calling on the people
to make away with stealers of children,
etc. The Sisters of Charity had received
many warnings of their peril from native
Christians and a few Europeans; moreover, many of the children under their
care who were not friendless orphans were
taken away by their families. The Sisters
insisted on removing to the " Concessions,"
a European who was lying ill in their
hospital, for fear he should incur any risk
of life; but they never thought of securing
their own safety. It was their duty to
remain at their post, and so steadily and
calmly did they pursue the daily routine
that neither children nor native under-
mistresses in the orphanage had an inkling
of the coming storm.

Already the persecution was breaking
forth, and was swiftly increasing among
the native Christians living in both town
and neighbouring villages. A catechist
was savagely beaten and dragged before the
Tche-shien (sub-prefect) of Tien-tsin. Next

an excellent Christian schoolmaster, who
happened to visit the town, was accused
of being a sorcerer, met with the same
treatment until, badly wounded at the
Ya-men, he was, after much opposition
on the part of the Tche-shien, released and
carried by two Chinese Catholics on a
stretcher into the mission station residence.
To his brother, Father Chevrier wrote:
"At this moment all the devils in hell
seem to be let loose at Tien-tsin.

"For the last fifteen days the most
ridiculous calumnies have been spread and
believed about the Sisters. The Christians
will soon be exterminated, and I hope we
shall be at the head of them. One of my
best catechists was brought to me yesterday
in a basket quite naked, covered with blows
and wounds and quite unrecognisable, and
with a broken thigh. It is impossible for
me to tell you all or even half of what
happens here every day."

Again, to the Vicar-General, Father
Chevrier, five days before his own violent
death, wrote: "One of the fresh rumours
to-day is that two of our best catechists
are in despair because the pagans have
killed the wife of one and the daughter
of the other. To-day, Corpus Christi,
there were hardly any women at Mass.
The pagans, who were our friends, have
been made to believe that all Christians
are bad. To-day I tried to prove to them

that they were only too happy. *Beati
estis quum maledixerint vobis propter me.
Gaudete, et exsultate quoniam,* etc.*

"But this doctrine does not easily enter
into their minds. I was asked just now
if I did not fear for our establishments,
as large bodies of men were organised to
bring about a rising. I replied that our
only confidence was in God."

After an angry interview between the
Tche-shien and the French Consul, the
missionaries who did not share M.
Fontanier's conviction about the in-
violability of the French flag—that it
would be respected by a fanatical Chinese
mob out to murder the foreigners—were
now certain that their hours were numbered,
and that martyrdom was fast approaching.
Father Chevrier meeting a Frenchman in
the Chinese quarter of Tien-tsin told him,
"Come to-morrow to hear Mass; it is time
to prepare for death."

* Matt. vii. 12.

CHAPTER VII

THE CROWN OF GLORY

On the 19th and 20th of June the gongs and tom-toms were beating through the Chinese part of Tien-tsin, and tradesmen were closing their shops near the doomed Jen-tse-t'ang and carrying away all their goods, while the mandarins, who were secretly conniving at this state of unrest and disturbance, sent word to the Sisters that they would visit their establishment on the 21st June, to assure themselves that all was in order so that they could calm the excited people.

When this hypocritical message reached the Jen-tse-t'ang in the evening of the 20th, Sister Andreoni called together the children of the Sisters to put everything in good order. She also told them that in consequence of this official visit they would dine at ten instead of eleven as usual. Some of the children were frightened and began to cry. "Come," said the Sister, giving to each of them a pretty picture, "if you have faith in God there is nothing to fear." Then the night prayers were said as usual, and everyone went to bed. At that very moment, M. Favier

wrote, the organiser of the massacre warned
all the shopkeepers in the neighbourhood
of the Sisters' house not to open their
shops the next day, and to fill their
" kangs " (large varnished water pots
placed in the court of every house) with
water, so that the firemen on their arrival
should find the supply ready and be able
at once to stop the incendiary flames
should they spread to adjoining houses.
The next morning the Sisters rose at their
usual early hour, attended to their religious duties, heard Mass, received Holy
Communion, and passed the morning in
their respective avocations.

Meanwhile Father Chevrier heard the
confessions of many Christians " till the
moment when the big bell of the church
rang the last time for the parochial
Mass.   Before going up to the altar Fr.
Chevrier had the happiness of receiving
Mr. de Coutris, who, according to his
promise the evening before, had come to
prepare himself for death by hearing
holy Mass and making a good Communion.
After the Mass was over peace still reigned,
and the missioners could go quietly to
their breakfast.   Towards nine o'clock the
doomed Missionaries, Priests and Sisters,
could hear the ominous gongs being
vehemently beaten in the town, where the
men of the fire brigades, the revolutionary
and fierce " Y-min," or Voluntaries,

together with many soldiers, the riff-raff,
and scum of Tien-tsin, assembled under the
command of the wicked old Tai-Ping chief.

This unruly mob collected first in front
of the Lazarist Fathers' mission and the
French Consulate, where, in the course of
the day, they massacred the priests, Fathers
Ou and Chevrier, the French Consul,
several other French and Russian subjects,
besides setting on fire the Consulate, the
mission station, and the church. Meanwhile, the Sisters of Charity, writes our
author, " were preparing themselves for
a speedy death. Their mortal agony had
been long and cruel. Since they left the
chapel in the morning they had been able
to breathe for a few hours in peace. Before
nine o'clock, however, an unknown woman,
of sinister looks, came into the hospital and
examined everything without speaking.
The people about the place thought she
had been probably sent by the heads of
the insurrection to convince themselves
that the Sisters had no means of defence.
Anyhow, it alarmed them all, and when the
gong sounded in that quarter at nine
o'clock they thought themselves lost. They
heard a tremendous uproar and the savage
cries of the mob, but by degrees the storm
seemed to abate, and a relative silence
prevailed in their house."

Though they were mercifully preserved
by Divine Providence from hearing any

details of the horrible events taking place
at the mission station and French Consulate, the Sisters knew that their end
was only a matter of a few hours. For,
"from the belvedere above, they could
see that the crowd was wending its way
to the French Consulate, and the mission
house. Rather reassured, as far as they
were themselves concerned, they thought
most of the dangers to which the poor
missioners would be exposed. Poor
Sisters ! so devoted to their holy Director
and Father Ou ! (their Chinese chaplain),
these voluntary exiles of charity thought
themselves lost in a town full of demons.
By that time Father Chevrier and his
colleague Father Ou, their bodies fearfully mutilated by the infuriated murderers, had already been thrown into the
river, while the Consulate and mission
station and church were set on fire—only
the cross and the inscription of Our Lady
of Victories escaping the flames."

At the Jen-tse-t'ang, according to the
report of a Chinese woman, Tchae Marie,
who helped Sister Andreoni in the care
of the orphans, this good Sister took the
children into dinner, saying, to reassure
them : " You must not be afraid. If really
they want to kill some one, it will only be
the Sisters ; for you Chinese there is no
danger, it will not affect you."   Although
the Sister spoke thus bravely, added

Tchae Marie, " one saw that she was very
anxious. She seemed ill, and walked with
difficulty. That day they had prepared a
dish for the children which they liked very
much ; but no one was disposed to eat,
which the Sister seeing, did all in her power
to reassure them. Saddened even unto
death, the poor Sisters of Charity went
from time to time to shed tears before the
Tabernacle of their Divine Spouse, and to
renew to Him the offering of their lives for
His love. But before their sick, their
orphans, and their little children they
remained firm and strong, like their holy
mother on Calvary. Only that day they
called together all those employed in the
house to go into the chapel and to pray to
Our Lord to appease the tempest which
raged against the missioners and the
Sisters."

So the hours wore on that hot day in
June, and the Sisters had, as usual, just
finished their spiritual reading when a
servant announced that from the belvedere
of the Jen-tse-t'ang could be seen the
flames issuing from the mission station
and the church. The Superioress, Sister
Marquet, ordered everyone into the chapel,
in the crypt of which were placed the
babies of the crèche. Then the doors were
locked as the cries of the approaching mob
over the bridge of boats were heard. The
Sister Sacristan hid the monstrance,

chalice, and cruets in the orphans' dormitory, where they were afterwards found. Meanwhile, the children began to sing the Litany of the Blessed Virgin in Chinese, and the Sisters knelt on the altar steps to receive their Viaticum from the hand of their Superioress, who, to preserve the Sacred Hosts from sacrilegious profanation, consumed the remainder left in the ciborium with Sister Andreoni.

They had scarcely completed their sacred office when the house door was forcibly broken in by the infuriated blood-thirsty mob, just fresh from their atrocious work at the mission house and Consulate. Sister Marquet quietly placed the pyx inside her habit over her chest, and intrepidly stood before the chapel to make a supreme effort to save the children, who, she thought, would be massacred with the Sisters. There she could hear the mob wrecking everything in the dispensary in their mad search for the children's eyes and hearts, which, they asserted, were used as drugs by "the white devils," while others were engaged in maltreating the porter of the convent so terribly that he died of his wounds some weeks later. Then they rushed to the inner court, where the chapel was situated. On their appearance Sister Marquet turned to the leader, saying calmly, "What do you want with us? We only try to do all the good we can to your poor

and sick. If you wish for our lives, here
we are, all ten of us ; we are ready to die ;
but spare, at least, our poor children."

This dignified and touching appeal made
no impression on these Chinese fiends, who
instantly cut open her head with a sabre,
killing her ; and then they murdered Sister
Andreoni, who was standing near. Some
of the mandarin's servants or Yamen
runners who were in the mob, told the
Christian prisoners that they had noticed
a bright light on Sister Marquet's breast,
from which they saw some lovely children
flying upwards to the roof of the chapel.

While this martyrdom was going on
two of the other Sisters went into the
crypt with the orphans, and Sister Alice
O'Sullivan and five of her companions
left the chapel by the side doors, in the
hope, no doubt, that by exposing their
lives they might thereby save those of the
children. Sister O'Sullivan having come
out by a door not far from the kitchen,
the murderers seized a saucepan of boiling
water and scalded her fearfully. In her
agony she ran towards the chapel, and was
killed there near her Superioress.

Her death, though painful and shocking
enough, was, however, merciful in com-
parison to the tortures inflicted on three
of the other Sisters, one of whom had her
eyes and heart torn out before her death
amid the jeers of her barbarous murderers,

while two others were literally roasted
over a fire, though it is hoped that they were
killed previously.   Nameless barbarities
we are told, were inflicted on the mangled
remains of these ten defenceless women,
and before three o'clock these holy souls
had all gone to claim the martyr's crown,
It was stated by the pagans that as the
massacre was going on the wife of a bonze
or heathen priest, was watching the terrible scene fron her balcony, and as each
Sister expired she beheld a brilliant cloud
soaring up into heaven. She was so impressed with this prodigy that she exclaimed
that these people must have been dear
friends of God, and she ran over to the
Sisters' courtyard. On being asked what
brought her there she said they were
killing holy people, and that she had come
to adore the God of the murdered Sisters.
One of the rabble at once cut off her head
and in her baptism of blood the poor ignorant soul went to join the martyrs' glorious
band.

Though the Chinese official report said
that 100 children were asphyxiated in the
crypt of the chapel where two Sisters had
taken them, the missionaries thought that
there were only twenty who shared the
fate of their kind guardians. For it is
known that the ruffians, as soon as they
had completed their odious murders, collected all the children and had them

brought to the Yamen of the sub-prefect, who had been so active in bringing about this attack upon the mission station and French Consulate. Here six mandarins who " sat in the seats of honour," reported the heroic Tchae Marie (who had escaped being killed by her fiendish countrymen), " one after the other questioned us, asking each how and why we had come to the Jen-tse-t'ang ? The children answered simply and clearly as to the causes of their coming to the Sisters, the village from which they had been brought, and the names of the people who brought them. They one and all declared that it was their parents who had brought them to the orphanage, that they had never been bewitched or carried off by force of any sort, and that the papers existed, written by the authorities of each village, when each child was admitted into ' the House of Mercy.' The judges then called the little boys, whom they took on their knees, giving them sugar-plums and trying to coax them by caresses, saying, ' Where do you come from ? ' etc., but all these little fellows answered like the others."

Thus out of the innocent mouths of these grateful children, girls and boys alike, the charitable and kind missionaries who had done so much for them, were amply vindicated, despite the blandishments of the artful pagan mandarins. One boy having

5

been asked what he read at the Jen-tse-t'ang, bravely began to repeat the ten commandments and some of the catechism until interrupted by his questioner. The more ·the children were tormented by Yamen satellites to say that the Sisters tore out the eyes and hearts of some of their companions, the more did the heroic children protest that these reports were all calumnies and lies. That these little confessors for the Faith, imprisoned in roofless barns, with only scanty food allowed them by their jailers, were visibly protected by God, was proved by the extra-ordinary fact that one day when a violent storm was raging, not one drop of the heavy rain fell upon the poor helpless children, so that the astonished heathens cried out, " The Christian religion must be the true one. See how these children are protected." When the children were given back to the new missionaries who were sent to replace the martyred priests, out of one hundred and twenty, about a hundred and one were by degrees restored to the Catholic orphanage.

As for the much mutilated remains of the Sisters of Charity, it was quite true that the Chinese miscreants threw them into the fire at the Jen-tse-t'ang, from whose charred ruins the few carbonised bones of the poor Sisters were reverently collected. These were solemnly interred

on August 3rd, in a grave on the site of
the destroyed mission station, in the presence of an immense crowd, among whom
were the native and foreign high officials
and all the foreign residents in the Tien-tsin
Concession. Mgr. Thierry, the Pro-Vicar
of Chi-li, who conducted the funeral service,
in his oration observed that "the death
of the victims had been to them a gain ;
coming to China with a hope of martyrdom, they had attained the accomplish-
ment of their sincere wish, and had given
their lives for Jesus Christ."

It may be remarked here that as soon
as "the news of the martyrdom became
known in all the houses of the Sisters of
Charity, more than three hundred of them
entreated earnestly the favour of being
allowed to go and replace their companions who had died so gloriously in the
field of honour."

Fr. Etienne, the fourteenth Superior-
General of the Mission, after the first
moments of his bitter grief were over,
exclaimed, "Blessed be God. I may now
sing my *Nunc dimittis*, and die in peace,
for I, too, have martyrs among my
children."

As for the wicked city of Tien-tsin,
where the actual criminals were left un-
pun shed for their villainous deeds, on
the first anniversary of the massacres a
fearful inundation--said to have been pre-

dicted by Father Chevrier on his apparition to some pagans after his death—
ruined the crops and the whole country-
side, destroyed houses, and drowned from
about two to three thousand people. Even
"the Chinese looked upon these misfortunes as a sign of the Divine wrath
on account of the massacres." Every
year saw similar floods, while famine,
cholera, typhus, plague, etc., have not
been spared the guilty town and its inhabitants. In 1877 a terrible fire broke
out, and of four thousand women and
children only six hundred escaped with
their lives from the flames in the south-
east part of the city. It is known that the
mandarins who connived at the murders
of the Tien-tsin martyrs all met with
various misfortunes and had very un-
happy deaths.

Over forty-seven years have passed
away since the heroic daughters of St.
Vincent de Paul underwent their cruel
martyrdom. The few remains left of them
have long rested in their quiet grave under
the shadow of the wrecked church. Rebuilt
though it was, yet during the Boxer rebellion in 1900 it probably fell again under
the terrific cannonade that reduced the
Chinese town of Tien-tsin to a heap of
stones. Yet the saintly Sisters have
not been forgotten by their friends or
the Catholic Church, for whose sacred

doctrines they worked as true apostolic labourers in the Chinese mission field. When some Chinese martyrs of a much older period were beatified some time ago, the little Irish Sister Alice O'Sullivan was still well remembered by her warm-hearted countrymen, who, thinking she had been included in this beatification, illuminated her birthplace, the old town of Clonmel, on the bank of the Suir, to testify their joy and pride in the honour which we believe will eventually be paid by the Church to the name of the gentle Sister, the daughter of St. Vincent de Paul and St. Patrick. To her may be applied the words of Apocalypse when it speaks of those " who are come out of great tribulation, and have washed their robes, and have made them white in the blood of the Lamb " (Ch. vii. 14).

CHAPTER VIII

A TRUE SON OF ST. PATRICK

THE place of honour in this volume was
naturally given to the Martyr of Clonmel,
quite independently of all chronological
reasons. But we have now to tell the
simple story of another soul gifted to
China by Tipperary—one who was a true-
hearted Irishman, a good priest, and in
his quiet way a great missioner of Christ.
It has been frequently said that it is well
nigh impossible to get Irishmen to devote
themselves to the work of converting the
pagans of the Far East. We look upon
this as a grievous calumny on the apostolic
faith and the devotion of Irish Catholics.
All that is needed is to bring home to them
the necessities of the case, and they will
not be wanting to their duties or to their
opportunities. But no motive for moving
the hearts of the students in our ecclesiastical colleges can be more effectual than
to bring before them the concrete case of
one who was once in their own position,
and who both offered himself generously
to this work, and was most successful in
prosecuting the grand object of his
ambition. Of Father Patrick Moloney it

70

can be said most truly, "Consummatus in brevi, explevit tempora multa."

Our attention was first called to the striking career of the subject of this sketch by the following extract from the letter of one who has nobly devoted a life's labour to the poor Chinese. Writing from Ning-po, in August, 1898, our correspondent said :—

"There formerly laboured in China an Irish missionary, Father Moloney, who was much beloved by the natives, and died, after St. Francis Xavier's style, alone in a boat, with a couple of native attendants, miles away in the interior. The Chinese still talk of him, and according to his servants, Our Lady appeared to her devoted client to comfort him, and to show him the crown awaiting him. He was a great friend of M. Dauverchain, who always hopes to see more Irish priests working on the mission. I forward him the *Sheaf* and the *Irish Catholic*, as he is keenly interested in all you are doing. He is so grateful for the prayers asked, and so am I."

This Père Dauverchain was himself a very great missioner. He was the right-hand man of his Bishop, Monseigneur Reynaud, of Ning-po, marked by immense experience and the most fiery zeal. At a later period he was attacked by the Boxers, cruelly mishandled, and only escaped with his life because they believed they had done their work thoroughly, whereas he had merely swooned. When he came back to life and had recovered from the wounds inflicted upon him, he announced his recovery in the words, " Now I am ready for the Boxers once more."

This good priest had the greatest admiration for Father Moloney's zeal and apostolic qualities, and frequently said that no greater blessing could accrue to China than a supply of missionaries from the South of Ireland, provided they were of Father Moloney's type. When he heard, in the year 1898, that there was a movement started in Ireland promoted by *St. Joseph's Sheaf* to come to the help of China, he wrote to the editor :—

" I bless St. Joseph for the prosperity of your good work, all the more because we had here once a young Irish missionary, Patrick Moloney, who did much good and left a great void among us. He had been ten years in China, had started missions in many places, knew the spoken language very well, and was very fond of the natives, who were devoted to him in return. In the month of January, 1882, when on that mission, he caught the disease which we call *le charbon* in his face, and seeing himself in danger of death, sent for a priest, who started to help him, but having had more than 200 miles to travel, arrived after he had died. How happy

PATRICK MOLONEY.
As a Student at Thurles College

we should be if Providence could send
someone to replace him even now! He
died in the district of Kin-te-tchien, which
is the town for the manufacture of china,
with its millions of inhabitants. I love
to invoke Father Moloney as the patron
of this town, to bring down on it the
blessings of heaven."

In the year 1910 a correspondent wrote
from Ning-Po, "Father Dauverchain,
though old and very deaf, is still in
Kiang-si, and still hopes before he dies to
see a countryman of the heroic Irish priest of
former days labouring in the district where
Father Moloney met his saintly death."

Through the kindness of the same
devoted friend and colleague, we have
been supplied with a copy of a letter
written at the time of his death by
Father Moloney's Bishop, Monseigneur
Bray, who is now an aged prelate of
eighty years, and who requested and received the assistance as Coadjutor Bishop
of one who took a great interest in the
first beginnings of St. Joseph's Young
Priests, namely, Mgr. Ferrant, of Che-Kiang.

It has been the constant aim of this
Society, from its commencement, to bring
the needs of Catholic China clearly before
Irish readers, in order to arouse and
strengthen a desire in their hearts to
come to the assistance of our poor, struggling co-religionists of this arduous mission.

For this reason, if for no other, we are
extremely pleased to be in a position to
give a connected, if short, account of the
life and holy death of our noble-hearted
countryman, who left behind him, amongst
Chinese, quite as much as amongst his
own confrères, an undying memory of his
priestly virtue and Irish pluck.

On the west side of County Tipperary,
where the regular contour of the premier
county is broken into by the neighbourly
incursion of adjoining Limerick, a range
of rugged hills rises to a considerable
height, though overtopped on the south
by the more celebrated range of the Galtees.
The contrast between this mountainous
district and the rich lowlands lying only
a few miles distant is extreme ; and the
conditions of life are naturally very different. The inhabitants of the mountains are,
if not rough, a very sturdy breed ; and one
visiting the farms and surroundings of the
uplands will easily realise that the future
missioner of Kiang-si could not have been
reared in a more suitable environment.

It was here, then; on the slopes of the
townland of Corroughmarka (which is on
the very edge of County Tipperary, for
it belongs to the Parish of Doon in the
County Limerick), that Patrick Moloney
first saw the light on the Feast of the
Epiphany, 1846. He came of a race of
farmers, rooted to the soil, among whom

there are few families but give to the Church of Catholic Ireland some of her most stalwart champions. The boy's mother, in particular, was of a most priestly race. It was her pride to relate to her children how, even in penal times, her family had not been wanting to the needs of their countrymen, and how they had overcome many a difficulty, as, for instance, her great grand-uncle had received Holy Orders in no more stately cathedral than a retired stone quarry!

With such traditions in the family, it need not surprise us if, in more peaceful times, it has given not merely innumerable priests, but also a bishop,* to the Catholic Church. In later years one of Patrick's younger brothers was studying for the priesthood, but died in the year 1875, when the subject of this notice was already at work in China ; and even in a younger generation there are some members of another brother's family who are devoting themselves to the service of the Church.

We might dwell here on the virtues of the missionary's mother, but that they will be best understood by Irish Catholics, who know what a mother's influence is, from the story of her dear son's life.

* The Right Rev. Maurice F. Burke, D.D., Bishop of the Diocese of St. Joseph, Mo., U.S.A., consecrated in the year 1887, is a first cousin of Father Moloney's mother.

However, we will mention one incident which will show Patrick's love of his mother. When he returned from France, during his studies, he was rather rudely informed of his mother's recent death by one who wrongly thought he had already heard the news. Strong man though he was, the shock caused him to swoon away, and he fell to the ground as one dead, before his informant could utter a word of apology.

The character he displayed in after years, in his grand though short career, was fully foreshadowed in his boyhood. Though remarkable, as we shall see, for humility, patience, and sweetness of disposition, he had an element of subdued passion in him which the astute Chinaman easily recognised, and he was delighted to be known among the enemies of the faith as " The Foreign Devil." Now, one who knew him most intimately, as the companion of his boyhood, asserts that from his earliest years Patrick's character had something about it corresponding with what this name seems to imply. He was not merely manly, but fearless, and being fond of fun, did not always keep clear of scrapes. However, when he had deserved punishment, he did not always get it, for such a little favourite was he with all around him, that even the very servants about his father's place tried to shield him from his wrathful parents. His fault lay often with his tongue—"whatever was in, was out "—— and, added to this, he could give as good a "knuckling" as anyone else to a lad of his own size.

But if he had in his body a pure drop of Irish blood, he had the gift of pure Irish faith well planted in his soul. This was seen when he was sent, at the early age of fifteen, to the Jesuit School of the Sacred Heart in Limerick ; for, though he was quite free to follow his own bent, our informant, who was in lodgings with him, says even now he cannot forget the lesson taught him by the honest fervour of this little schoolboy. Every morning he was up and in the chapel hearing Mass, and at night he would kneel down by the bedside, pouring out his young heart to the Mother of God, whom he loved most tenderly. His cousin thinks that often he must have occupied fully three-quarters of an hour in reciting his Rosary and other prayers.

The boy is father to the man, and how can we wonder if such a boy as this, manly, reliable, devoted to his duty, should, when he reached manhood, rise to the level of his opportunity, and do great things for God and his fellow-men ?

Subsequently his parents sent him from the day-school at Limerick where he had

to be in lodgings, to reside as a boarder
at the College of Castleknock, near Dublin.
They merely intended to procure for him
a thoroughly high-class education; but
in reality this change of school appears to
have had a profound influence upon his
after life. Castleknock College is directed
by the Vincentian Fathers, and it is
probable that here he got the germ of
that vocation which developed later when
he was at the Irish College in Paris.

It was not, however, very long before
he expressed a wish to be a priest, which
cannot have surprised anyone, and he was
sent for his studies, in the natural course
of things, to the diocesan college of Thurles.
His parents thought that he would, like
many of his relatives, become a priest of
the Cashel diocese, to which his parish,
Doon, belongs. We may remark in passing
that Cashel has a peculiar glamour of its
its own. Like Tara of the North, it was
once a royal residence. It is known,
indeed, as the City of the Kings—there
Cormac reigned, and there is still seen
upon the famous Rock that Chapel which
bears Cormac's name (for he was Bishop
as well as King), and which is one of the
loveliest gems of the early style of
Christian architecture. Only a few miles
from the Rock is Holy Cross Abbey, where
was venerated the most important portion
of the True Cross belonging to the west

of Europe, credibly stated to have been
given by Godfrey, King of Jerusalem, to
his niece Queen Matilda.

We are sure that these things were
seen and felt by Patrick. Though Cashel
touched his southern soul (for he, too,
had a clear strain of romance in his com-
position), it was not destined to be his
except as a memory of the past.

He went to Thurles College in 1863,
and a year later he requested his parents
to send him to Paris, to the Irish College,
where again he would live under the
direction of the Vincentian Fathers, whom
he had learned to love. The request was
granted, and thus his friends were not
surprised to receive the news that he had
been admitted as a member of the Order.
And then something else happened to
Patrick. It was in Paris that he got the
grace to become a pioneer of Irish
missionaries, a true hero of Christian
fortitude and self-sacrifice, a martyr of
charity, almost a saint of the Catholic
Church. The little Thurles student had
not yet realised the destiny that Providence
had marked out for him as for a child of
special predilection. He had not, we
believe, been distinguished among his
fellow seminarians in Ireland, unless for
a certain simplicity in his adhesion to duty.
Little did he or his companions guess that
one day his name would be pronounced

with benediction by generations of Irish
students yet unborn, aye, and in many
a Catholic home in the far distant realm
of the Celestial Empire!

But God's ways are often strange, and
never more than in His silent workings in
those souls whom He has marked for His
own. It was in Paris that God's grace
worked in Patrick's soul like leaven in
a batch of dough. The Congregation of
the Mission was founded by St. Vincent de
Paul to instil into the priests and Levites
of the Catholic Church a true spirit of
piety and apostolic zeal. From the
Vincentian Fathers Patrick had learned
at first-hand the truth about the Chinese
Empire, its vastness, its strange civilisation, the amiable and docile spirit of the
people, their state of utter abandonment
to a specially corrupt and degraded
paganism, their adaptability for con-
version, and their grit in withstanding the
most terrible forms of persecution or
torture.

This information sank into the good
soil of Patrick Moloney's heart, and, like
the good seed, there it remained, and
germinated, till one day it brought forth
its hundredfold of golden grain. The
process was slow but sure. He ruminated,
debated with himself, prayed to God for
light and help, and finally resolved to act.
At first he merely viewed the matter in

FATHER DANVERCHAIN, C.M.
Fr. Patrick Moloney's friend.

a general sort of way, asking himself—If
the facts are these, if there is such a grand
field open to Irish zeal, if there is a special
demand for Irish missioners in China, why
is it that Irishmen always stand aloof
from the great undertaking ?   He knew
that Frenchmen were giving themselves
yearly, almost daily, to the task of converting the Chinese to the Faith of Christ
—he knew that many other nationalities,
though not in such numbers, were doing
some part of the work—and the thought
began to haunt him, why not Irishmen
also ? Why do they of all the nations
most   neglect   the   great   opportunity ?
Could not an Irishman, then, be a hero ?
Was he alone bereft of enthusiasm, of
devotion, of manly pluck ?

Then one day the thought came to him
(was it not as he received the broken
Body and the poured-out Blood of the
Redeemer ?) if the work is to be undertaken, if someone is to begin, and, if
someone must be the first to grasp the
nettle, it might perhaps be even Myself.
Then, for a moment, the thought came
that such an idea might possibly betray
a want of humility. He was a very
ordinary person, a merely average schol-
astic, and how could he presume to come
forward as a pioneer ? This was no
ordinary task, it would try the robustest
nature and might appal the stoutest

6

heart. To go forward when all his friends
and comrades, his forbears as well as the
present generation, had held back! So
he would disregard the inspiration, for
he did not yet know that this was of a
truth a divine call that was working in
his inmost soul. It was only when it
came back upon him, only when he found
it haunting him, urging him for the love
of Christ, that he determined to seek the
advice of others, and especially of his
confessor, as to whether he should not
volunteer for the missions of the Far East.

Help he undoubtedly gained where help
must be sought by Catholics when making
critical decisions,—but all the same what
a struggle yet lay before this poor lad
from Co. Tipperary. The call of home and
country could not be disposed of so easily.
He yearned for Ireland and for his flesh
and blood, who were waiting to have him
back with the sacred unction of the priesthood fresh upon him. *Cor ad cor loquitur.*
They had a share in his life, they had a
right to his devotion even as a minister
of Christ. He had yet to learn by experience the great lesson that the Creator
does not allow His creatures to outdo
Him in generosity—and that what they
give up for Him is returned to them in
full measure, well-shaken, pressed together
and pouring over into their bosom. It
seemed at first too great—this sacrifice of

all that was nearest and dearest, like parting with his own soul.

So it came about that two calls were tugging at his heart-strings—the call to Ireland and the call to China. " Tell him that I came from Tipperary," said a young student when asking an interpreter to explain his identity to a stiff Roman ecclesiastic, who did not know English, and seemed scarcely to have heard of Ireland! The call to Tipperary was undoubtedly strong ; but the call to China in the end prevailed.

It was the thought of those apostolic men who had shed a halo of glory over Catholic Ireland that steeled Patrick to make this supreme sacrifice, which seemed almost impossible ; but for which, after he had once made it, he never had a regretful moment. Next to the Mother of God and her spouse St. Joseph, he trusted most to the merits and intercession of his patron St. Patrick, of St. Columbkille, St. Columbanus, and all the long roll of the saintly apostles of Ireland. What they had done he, too, would try to do. What matter that his vocation was at that period an unusual one, would perhaps appear strange and extravagant to those he was going to abandon, as it might seem, for ever. So long as he knew that God would be with him, it was enough. Like Cardinal Newman, he could murmur in the depths of his soul " Guide Thou my feet; I do not ask to see the distant scene—one step enough for me."

The sequel to this story will prove to the reader that Patrick was not long in reaping his reward. He was ready to wait for heaven, but lo! in this life Divine Providence marked an approval of his sacrifice, and that within the bosom of his own family. Grace was about to touch a very near and very dear relative, and this time it was a woman who was chosen to be the willing victim for another grand sacrifice. His dear cousin would soon follow him on his long journey to the Far East—and in imitation of Father Patrick, and even joining the Vincentian Order, she too would like him reap a great reward, and bring great glory to their family and its native county. The reader is referred to the brief account of Mary Ryan's missionary labours given at the end of the present volume.

But the cross was mingled with his joy. The time for his ordination was approaching, and he was not to have the supreme happiness of offering the Holy Sacrifice for his parents during their life time. He was ordained in Paris, 1871, when he was just twenty-five years of age, and some years previously his father and mother had left this world. It was perhaps better so. He had volunteered for China, and very soon took his departure.

CHAPTER IX

WE have now to describe Father Moloney's
career as a missioner in the great Empire
to which he had devoted his life. Before
entering upon details, in order to enable
the reader to grasp the nature of the work
that lay before the young priest, it will be
desirable, at this point, to convey to him
some idea of the condition of China in
1871, that is, about a year subsequent to
the massacre of Tien-tsin, as described in
an earlier chapter. We shall, therefore,
quote rather freely from an important
document which was published in Belgium
about this time by George Ferguson, a
Catholic merchant, who had special opportunities for knowing the facts and who
wrote about them in a singularly sober
and judicious manner. That he was closely
in touch with the Catholic body may be
gathered from the fact that he had con-
ferred immense benefactions upon his own
mission of Chang-tong, which is a little to
the south of Che-li, in which province
Tien-tsin is situated. His generous dona-
tions, including land, a mission-house,
with provisional chapel (for which he was

85

about to substitute a larger church), are
described in *Les Missions Catholiques*, of
March, 1874, where it is also added that by
his writings he has rendered an apostolic
service not so much to one mission in
particular as to all the missions of China.

The pamphlet, entitled *Aperçu de la
Situation en Chine* (1873), naturally deals
with politics and economic and military
matters as well as with religion—these
questions being often so closely related in
the Celestial Empire that it is very difficult
to consider any one of them independently
of the others. Mr. Ferguson (who was
generally classed as an Englishman, but
may have been Irish by birth) maintains
that at the date of writing it was clearly
the policy of the Chinese Government to
close all the ports (and especially Tien-tsin)
to European traders, with the sole excep-
tion of Shanghai, where their interests
were too safe to be attacked. He also
complains that "European diplomacy has
suffered more than one check in its praise-
worthy efforts to ameliorate the position
of the peoples concerned in it. In review-
ing the diplomatic transactions of the past
ten years, the Chinese may congratulate
themselves that they have yielded nothing
to representations made by the pleni-
potentiaries as to carrying out fully and
vigorously the spirit of the treaties which
have been made."

Speaking then of the recent massacres of Tien-tsin, the writer proceeds :—

"This horrible crime was precisely perpetrated by a crowd of people who knew little about Europeans, and were driven to the act of violence by their leaders for political motives, which were craftily hidden under a false zeal touching a wide-spread apprehension about the increase of population. To excite the people the more, they had been made wrongly to believe that the Europeans had been slaying their infants with a view of gradually destroying the Chinese race. If the people of Tien-tsin had possessed a sufficient knowledge of the charitable work against which they had been stupidly aroused by these perverse intriguers they would never have committed the barbarities which were really the result of their ignorance."

The writer then proceeds to explain another reason for the desire to keep strangers out of the country. It is merely a result of the natural isolation of China from the rest of the world, founded on a pitiful notion that it alone possesses all that there is in creation of law, intelligence, · and well-being. The Chinese are indeed beginning to know that the belief is not tenable, but they still shrink from granting that other nations are more advanced than their own, or that elsewhere people can be

as happy and as well-governed as they are
in the Middle Empire.

"But," he proceeds, "we ought to be
just, and we must admit that it is not only
the fault of the Chinese that we have not
advanced further in the path of inter-
national relations with them. The principles which governed the negotiations regarding Treaties in 1860 had established a
condition which it was simple to understand
and which would have brought matters to
a successful termination. It is the forget-
fulness of these principles in conducting
subsequent negotiations which has brought
about the actual situation. One can see
by the correspondence officially published
by the various Governments that expe-
diency has taken the place of fundamental
principles, and that these have ceased
even to be accounted as the basis of inter-
national relations.

"The reasons alleged by the Chinese
against a free entrance into their country
prove that it would be easier than is generally believed for the European Powers to
retrace their steps in the discussion of this
matter. Whenever they refuse any concession by alleging that it is not explicitly
stipulated in the Treaties, they never base
their refusal on the injustice of the demand,
but they accompany it by a recital of the
inconveniences which would result from a
concession. Now it would be easy to prove

to them that none of these alleged inconveniences would follow from a reasonable interpretation of the spirit of the Treaties."

Again, he says, on the same subject : "The Powers who in signing the Treaties with China had the honour of representing Christianity, do not appear to attach sufficient importance to the help which Christian maxims would afford in their transactions with Pekin, if only their Cabinets would apply the same. The conduct of those who were implicated in the massacre of Tien-tsin as also in the murder of the Tai-ping Chiefs after promising the British Commander that their lives would be secure, proves the lack of good principles among the Chinese authorities. The foreign Governments could not fail to be the gainers if, in order to bring home to the minds of the Chinese the principles of truth, honour, and fidelity to promises, they should obtain further facilities for the free propagation and free adoption of the Christian religion throughout the Empire.

"It is chiefly because the Chinese are pagans that they are so exclusive ; and it is strange, but yet true, that the Powers, in seeking to treat with China on a footing of equality, act as though they had very little to say to the Christians. Recently the Chinese Government manifested a desire to limit the rights of the Catholic

missioners regarding religion by means
of new agreements; but fortunately for
China the Powers firmly refused to sanction
any change in this legislation.   One is the
more surprised at such a proposal, because
recently the late Viceroy at Nanking,
Tseng-Quo-Fan, in a memorial, which he
presented two years ago to the Emperor,
insists upon the uselessness of his occupying
himself concerning the progress of Christianity in China, seeing that Confucianism
is so invulnerable that the authorities ought
to show their complete indifference to the
preaching of all other creeds."

Further down the writer proceeds :—

" A great misfortune for the missionaries
is that the Chinese Government has always
believed that they desire to propagate some
national religion instead of one which is
professed in common by all the Christian
peoples. To the Chinese religion means
a complex of social rules—therefore, the
introduction of a foreign cult always seems
to them to amount to an innovation favour-
ing some particular people. So they try
to conclude that it is the aim of Christianity
to acquire some political or territorial influence for the nation to which the missionaries belong.

" For example, the Catholic religion is
always now represented to be an institution
that is peculiarly French, while Protestantism is viewed as a kind of Confucianism

which is established in England and
America. Catholic missioners, even when
Italians, Belgians, Spanish, or Portuguese,
are considered to be really French* ;
and it would be extremely difficult to per-
suade the natives that English or Ameri-
cans are true Catholics. The mere fact
that two different forms of Christianity are
offered to the Chinese appears to the
Chinese as something very paradoxical, for
they do not know enough history to realise
that Protestantism is a recent form of
Christianity, resulting from a departure
from the ancient church ; and it would
appear to them still more incredible that
England had ever been Catholic or that
among the subjects of Great Britain and
America there are millions who profess that
religion.

· "The reason of this is that the policy
of the Legations of these two peoples has
always been to identify themselves exclusively with Protestantism although they
still represent such Catholic populations.
This belief regarding the Christian religion
has produced very bad effects. The idea
that Catholicism is merely a French religion
induces the Chinese to believe that the
opposition they offer to it will never cause
any provocation capable of interesting
Great Britain or America. The massacre

* Probably this means that they use chiefly the
French language when speaking to the Chinese.

at Tien-tsin has provided an instance well
fitted to confirm this unfortunate idea.
Among the victims was an Irish Sister of
Charity, and the British Government de-
clined taking any part in the demand for
reparation, leaving to the French Government the task of arranging the matter
' in globo ' along with that of the French
Sisters.   In so acting, the English Legation
merely acted in conformity with its traditions, with the view of avoiding to commit
itself to the idea that it could be possible
for Great Britain to be in any way Catholic.

"This cannot go on indefinitely, for
undoubtedly before long the Catholics of
Great Britain, of the United States, and
of Germany will desire to share with other
nations the honour and the merit of converting China, and English, American,
and German Catholic missioners will appear
in the Middle Empire. The more the
establishment of Catholic missions in China
shall be hastened by English, American,
and German missioners, the more assured
we shall be of the success of the Gospel of
Christ in this country."

So far, Mr. Ferguson, and finally as a
striking proof of his statements as to the
aims of the mandarins, he quotes a long
document which had been widely circulated at least with their connivance, among
the ignorant Chinese. It is too long to
transcribe here fully, but we may give the

substance of it with a few extracts. It is entitled " Important and Necessary Undertaking for the Salvation of the Empire." After a historical introduction, it declares that never had the Empire been devastated in the past as it is to-day by the Europeans, who have brought upon it the most cruel calamities. The first question dealt with is the opium trade ; then the priests—the Fathers who under the pretext of preaching virtue in reality seduce simple-minded folk ; their sermons are composed of obscene words and brutal aspirations. Men and women assemble together in the same churches, thus treading under their feet all the laws of morality.

" But (we now give the text) what is a still greater crime and truly worthy of death is that they are resolved to overthrow the three religions which are admitted in the Empire, and to upset even the altars of the great god Tu-hoang himself. The founder of their religion was an ancient barbarian named Jesus, whose Cross they place in the midst of their temple. They tear out the eyes of the sick man at the point of death, and send them to the Kingdoms of the West, pretending to make of them a sovereign remedy.

" Now since the mandarins of different localities could with difficulty head such an undertaking it is to you, men of the country and of merchandise, that we address these

secret instructions. Will you allow these
Europeans to overthrow the Empire with
their wickedness! If you think that we
are led into error and speech contrary to
the truth you will soon witness the Chinese
Empire plunged into barbarity. A tardy
repentance will rend our heart, our hands
will fall helpless, tears will deluge our
cheeks. Let us at once destroy these
wolves and panthers. Let us overthrow
the power of iniquity to preserve our honour
and our rights!''

We trust the reader has not been wearied
by the length of the above extracts, which
seemed to the writer to be very useful for
our purpose. It is not often that one
finds in the space of a single document so
much clear and really first-hand information as to the conditions ruling the Chinese
missions at the very moment of Father
Patrick Moloney's arrival in the country.
With it the reader will find himself able to
form a very clear notion of the position in
which he and his colleagues found themselves at a period removed by almost a
half-century from our time. Without it
he would probably have been at a loss to
understand many an expression in Father
Moloney's letters home, which it will be
now his privilege to peruse.

The special mission to which Father
Moloney was assigned was Kiang-si, which
at the time was a single Vicariate, though

subsequently divided into the three Vicar-
iates of North, South, and East Kiang-si.
He arrived at his field of work just before
Christmas in the year 1871.

The qualities of the missioner would be
here put to the test, for it is a peculiarly
hard mission, being not on the coast, but in
the interior of the country, and thus more
removed from the influence and the safe-
guards of European intercourse. His first
duty, naturally, was to endeavour to
familiarise himself with the language of the
race to whose eternal interests he had come
to devote his life. It is a curious circumstance, and one that says much for his
perseverance, that, although he became
later a most accomplished and fluent
speaker of the Chinese language, at first he
found the difficulty of its attainment
almost insuperable. However, even at this
early period of his ministry, he went with
his Bishop, Monseigneur Bray, on a tour to
the west of the enormous diocese, and
though he had much difficulty in making
himself understood, yet he devoted himself
with great ardour to the work of the con-
fessional and of catechising the young.

At a very early period of his missionary
career, another obstacle harassed him in
his work. When at Lin-Kiang, the change
of climate and of manner of life brought
on him an internal disorder which caused
him the acutest suffering, and brought

him into the very jaws of death. The
Bishop states that when he saw him (for
they had been separated) he found him so
shockingly reduced that he was unable to
restrain his tears at the sight, for he thought
he was going to lose his promising young
missioner.   But it was not so ordered, for
most fortunately a Scotch doctor happened
to be within reach, who was extremely kind
and attentive to Father Moloney, and soon
brought him round to a state of con-
valescence. One return of the malady
threatened him in the following year,
but it was less sharp and of shorter duration.
After his health was thoroughly established,
the Bishop, finding him to be pious,
humble, and affable, now determined to
send him away to a distant mission where
his zeal and his virtues could have full
scope in dealing with the poor people of
the country.

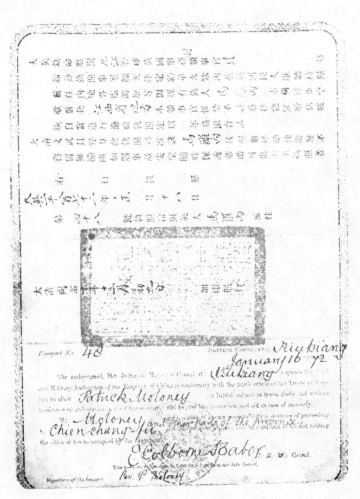

PATRICK MOLONEY'S PASSPORT TO CHINA.

CHAPTER X

LETTERS HOME

SOME of Father Moloney's letters which have reached us were written from the somewhat remote region to which it has been stated that he was sent very soon after his arrival in China. These will give us a more vivid idea of the man and of his work than any other source of information, so we transcribe them with pleasure.

By the kindness of his brother, we have been favoured with the loan of some letters which were written to his friends at home when he was on this mission. In one, written on April 8th, 1875, just after hearing the news of his brother's death, and asking for further particulars, of himself he writes: " I am as happy as you can wish me to be. I wish you all the same happiness. No doubt sometimes we meet with painful moments, but these are few, and to be compared to dark clouds that pass away and leave the sky more brilliant. To-morrow I shall begin a long journey of at least 300 miles, in a small boat covered over with a sort of bamboo leaves to protect us from the weather. I cannot tell the time it will take, but at least from

twenty to thirty days. . . . We have in this
province about 3,000 catechumens. Last
year there were about 400 adults baptised,
and I think we had from 4,000 to 5,000
little ones baptised—all getting a passport
for heaven, since they are the children of
pagans, baptised when in danger of death.
You see what a glorious mission I have.
Let us thank God and pray that I may
prove myself worthy of so noble a vocation.
Pray, and obtain prayers, for the con-
version of the idolaters, who are probably
more than double the population of Europe."

The following batch of letters has been
kindly forwarded to the writer by an uncle
of Father Moloney's, who, after his father's
death, in 1867, became guardian of the
family, and was, consequently, the recipient
of the missionary's correspondence.

It would not be possible, within our limits,
though it would be interesting to many,
to transcribe the whole of this correspondence which has come into our hands. But
before laying some extracts before our
readers we may here note that in several
particulars the letters confirm the estimate
formed of him by his Bishop in the memoir which came first into our hands and
formed the basis of our sketch.

One of the leading features of Father
Moloney's letters is the extreme tender-
ness of his affection to his kith and kin.
Though engrossed heart and soul in his

mission, with its arduous work, its danger
to his life, and its vast spiritual issues—
though cut off for ever from home, and
from all the ties of flesh and blood, his
mind is ever reverting to those he left
behind. At one time he is asking help of
their prayers for the success of his undertaking, at another time exhorting them to
the practice of all Christian virtue and
brotherly love, at another defending one
who had, without any fault of his own,
caused pain and discontentment to his
friends, and sometimes merely pointing
out, to one and all, the pure love of a
heart that has been chastened, indeed,
but not cooled, by prayer and the sacrifice
of a life. This is worth remarking, because
the idea of holiness which worldly people
form to themselves is, that it is cold and
repulsive, wanting in deep human love,
self-contained, and unsympathetic. It is
quite true that holiness has ideals and
standards of its own which are diverse
from those of the world—it is true that
the affections of the saints are unearthly
and transformed beyond what is natural
and common, but all the while they are
stronger than death and true as the purest
gold that has been burnt in the crucible.

Another quality of Father Moloney's,
which must strike the reader of his letters,
is not merely his devotion to his work,
but his extreme consolation and even joy-

fulness of heart in carrying it on. He says,
again and again, that he is happy to his
heart's content, as happy as the day is
long ; and this is the more remarkable if
we consider that in addition to the other
tremendous difficulties he had to contend
with, his health was not at all good.

Though the letters are mostly serious
enough, he sometimes betrays his gaiety
of soul by a little joke, as when he signs
himself nothing more than " Yours, Paddy
from Ireland," or makes allusion to his
littleness of stature—saying that he is
about the same size as John Chinaman,
but that his uncle must not conclude that
the latter are all Tom Thumbs. He is
always full of hope as to the result of his
labours and those of his brethren, and he
defends the Chinese character, praising
the constancy of the Christians, and saying
of the pagans that they are at least most
respectful, if not full of admiration, for
the work done by the Catholic missioners.
Again and again, he expresses a hope that,
perhaps, he may be called on to shed his
blood for the poor people ; a thing that at
one time did not appear improbable.

However, it is time that we should keep
our promise, and give a few, perhaps too
few, extracts from the letters.

In a letter, dated September 8th, 1873
(from Ling-Kiang-Pu), he writes :—

" May the love of the amiable Jesus be

ever in our hearts ! . . . China is divided
into eighteen provinces. That in which
I am is called Kiang-si, and is at least
twice as large as the green little Erin. Its
population is about twenty millions, and
there are about eighty large cities. The
Christian population consists of about
twelve thousand, with some thousand catechumens. There are, along with the Bishop,
twenty priests, only seven of whom are
European, all French, except one Italian,
and the little Irishman who is writing to
you. The rest are, of course, Chinese. We
have great hopes of numerous conversions
in the next few years. At present there are
twenty-five Chinese students in the Bishop's
College, who promise much to advance the
interests of Jesus and Mary. What we
specially want is prayers, for we have to
struggle againstthe ' Old Boy,' who is en-
raged at his losses. In two districts we
have had persecutions—the chapel being
burnt in one, and about forty Christian
families expelled from house and home.
Besides, a young Christian woman was
struck to death by her father-in-law and
mother-in-law, because she would not renounce her faith. In the other place the
Italian priest was wounded in the head,
and his clothes torn to pieces by the barbarous rabble of one of the great cities,
and all at the instigation of the civil magis-
trates ; at present he is getting better.

There was a man who wanted to embrace our holy religion, and so his friends tied his hands and hung him up for a whole day on a stage. Besides, he was flogged, with the consent of his wife and friends, and a short time after he died. Many Christians tried to get to see him, to baptise him, but in vain, though he always said he wished to become a Christian.

" There are a good many more incidents of the same character. Don't imagine that I am half dead here on account of what I am after relating. No such thing. On the contrary, the pagans fear us in many places. About the end of last year an entire little village embraced the faith ; the neighbours were afraid of them, and came and made presents of many things to us, in order that we may be friendly with them. When anything is against one Christian, all the others come to help him, and thus they frighten the pagans by their numbers and their loyalty to each other. Thus, ever dearest uncle and aunt, putting ourselves entirely in the hands of God and His Immaculate Mother, we are joyful and as happy as any mortal could wish to be. Even if we be so happy as to shed our blood for the love of Jesus, so much the better, even for the propagation of our holy faith, for we know that the blood of martyrs is the seed of Christians. I must finish for want of time, though I have many things to say.

Remember me to all cousins in Langhill, as also to all beyond the river, as well as to those at *the chapel*, at *the cross*, and in *the middle*. A fond adieu for the moment."

The next letter from which we quote was written in 1874, from Fou-chou-fou, after the illness to which we have already referred. He says :—

"Since I wrote to you, I was almost dead, being the second time I was dangerously ill since I came here. I was sick from September till January. About Easter I was able to go on the mission. When I arrive at a Christian settlement, I remain at a house for the time necessary to give them some instructions and hear their confessions. I am generally surrounded with numbers of open-mouthed spectators [pagans], who are most anxious to behold the 'foreign devil.' Millions of them regard us as kidnappers of little children, who pluck out their eyes for medicine, and even more hideous calumnies are widely propagated among the ignorant. We have the happiness of converting some hundreds, but not without the shedding of blood, whether missionary's, Christian's, or catechumen's. Last year there were two priests killed in the province of Su-Schuen. Here, in the Kiang-si, we have had a chapel burned, and two Christians murdered, etc. Do not, ever dearest uncle, forget your fond nephew in your prayers. Be not

afraid for my life. It is only when I am
dead that I will begin to live. Though
far from friends, I am as happy as you
could wish. I would not change for the
seat of the Emperor of the Celestial Empire,
as they call it."

In the following year he writes to his
brother :—

" I have, dearest Gerald, an extent of
land to evangelise as large as half Ireland,
and its population is at least equal to
that of Ireland. I am most happy, and
in good health. I have given some few
missions for the last eight months. Oh !
that we had some thousand good priests out
here ' to enlighten those who sit in the
shadow of death, and to direct their feet
into the ways of peace.' Pray, and ask
prayers of your fellow-students for the con-
version of China. We are daily exposed to
be the victims of our enemies ; but nothing
is to be feared by us, if we have God on our
side. Every day we have new converts.
The more we suffer, the more numerous
are the conversions. Thus raise your hearts
and hands towards the Queen of Mercy
for your poor but happy brother, and the
Chinese entrusted to his care."

In another letter, written previously to
the above, he gives an amusing account of
his own appearance, which we cannot re-
frain from transcribing :—

" I wear a long robe, like the Chinese,

very large, and buttoned at the side, like a soutane, but much looser about the body, a collar of paper, covered with silk or other stuff, about my neck; the head shaved, except the place where the Dominicans wear their tonsure, i.e., the crown. From this (all the rest being shaved) is suspended a bunch of hair, which sometimes reaches the heels. Those who, like me, have not hair long enough, wear a false *tail*, as we say, nicely plaited. Besides this I wear a pair of moustaches and a little beard (which are my own), a pair of linen stockings, shoes like slippers, having no strings, but each of two pieces to make the whole of it. So, if you did see me, I do not think you would recognise me. I am much the same as the Chinese as regards my size, and I am really much the same as if I had been here twenty years."

We have been favoured with yet another letter of Father Moloney, written from Kiang-si in the year 1874, addressed to his cousin, the French Sister of Charity, who died a most holy death at Ning-po, on the Feast of St. Francis Xavier, 3rd December, 1898.* It is full of interesting details as to his missionary life in the interior of China, and breathes, certainly not less than those of the two last batches, from which we quoted, a tender spirit of

* A further account of this nun (Sister Mary Ryan) is given in a later chapter of this vo ume.

piety, an ardent zeal for souls, and a deep
affection for his kindred. We have only
room for the following extracts :—

"Concerning you I have nothing more
to wish for. My desires are fulfilled, and
you are a daughter of St. Vincent. I congratulate you on your noble vocation to the
service of the poor. No doubt you feel
happy, being surrounded by so many white-
headed angels. Cherish your vocation more
than your life—thank Jesus at every moment for such an extraordinary privilege."

After referring in touching terms to a
member of his family who had recently
died, while a student at the College of
Thurles, saying, "I hope he casts a kindly
eye of tenderness on me in this my adopted
home of pagan China," and having referred
to many other members of his family, still
alive, he proceeds to speak of his own work:

"In order to make known to you my
position and my necessities, I will first
tell you how I am, and what I am doing.
I now, after two years, begin to speak the
language and at the beginning of this
month, I commenced a mission, being very
timid at first. But I put my confidence in
God and in His Immaculate Mother, and
so I began to preach and gave three
missions. I have still about twelve places
to visit, between this date (May 18th)
and the Feast of St. Vincent (July 19th).
Before starting on a mission I am obliged

to prepare everything requisite for the
Holy Sacrifice, even the wax candles. What
is more, we must carry our bedding with
us, otherwise we should have none.

"The first place I went to was a little
village of about one hundred families, only
five or six of them Christians. I found the
little house that they call the chapel.
Inside was a crucifix and a picture of our
amiable Mother, the walls black and dirty,
with no windows but a hole in the roof to
let in the light, and with it rain, snow,
or wind, if there is any. Beside the chapel,
a few small rooms, in one of which I took
up my abode, and the Christians did their
best to make me welcome. In that little
chapel, poor as it is, I was very happy,
being able to apply myself to all my
duties, without the least disturbance on
the part of the pagans, and I remained
there nearly a week. The next place I went
to was larger, but even less commodious,
and the house belonged partly to pagans.

"It is there the Christians recite their
prayers on Sundays only. Now, don't be
horrified at what I am going to tell you.
In the middle of this large hall, common
to all, there were to be seen the pictures
of our Divine Saviour and our Immaculate
Lady, and along with them some 'mon-
pans' or tablets in honour of the ancestors
of the pagans. They are about a foot in
length, and half as broad, being well

painted on wooden boards, and are altogether superstitious and diabolical, and
yet our Christians are obliged to have
them before them when they are saying
their prayers. . . . Here I was obliged to
prepare an altar, drawing a curtain before
the diableries, and getting it up as decently
as I could for the Holy Sacrifice of the
Mass. You will ask why I could not prepare one elsewhere ? Because there was
no other place. It would be impossible to
say Mass in the little rooms that belong
to the Christians, so miserable and filthy
are they, and the Christians are so poor
that it would be impossible for them to
build a little chapel, which would cost
about £50 or £60. However, if I remain
in the district, I shall ask the Bishop to
aid them, though he has at least thirty
or forty places which require his assistance more than this place, on account of
their numbers and importance. In that
same house there were twelve pagan
families. I was ever a spectacle to them,
and every day as I preached several of
them came to listen. Two embraced our
holy religion, and many others will come
into the fold, if you will pray well for
them. During the few days I was there,
I saw Chinese life : cursing and swearing
and other abominations from morning till
night. I assure you those who embrace
the faith will have many hard struggles

to undergo. Never did I see in a room so many black hoppers as I did in the one I was in there. No matter, I was happy, for I saw the action of grace on some good souls. After that I was happier than a prince, and it is only now that I begin to become a missionary. . . . We have some hundreds of conversions, and sometimes we have persecutions. A few days ago there were three Christians beaten to death, and others severely wounded. In another place one of our chapels was burned, and two Christians killed, besides several wounded. You see now how I am situated. Do you pray for me, and get others to pray. . . . You think I may be a martyr. It may be so, but I assure you it is a grace granted to few. I think I cannot aspire to it, for I cannot imagine that God would grant such an extraordinary grace to so worthless a creature. You imagine it is humility ? You do well, for we must all judge well of our neighbours ; but I assure you I am sincere, for now I have no secrets from you. It may be that I may be butchered one fine day, but not for the Faith, but as an espion (spy) belonging to the foreign devils, as we Europeans are called by the pagans. Come what will, if I am united to Jesus, it makes no matter."

These letters of Father Moloney, written only little more than two years after his arrival in China, are interesting, not merely

for the picture they give of his mission,
but because they enable us to see the
change it has already effected in his mind
and in his whole spiritual outlook. It is
not the ordinary growth which comes to
all young priests of good disposition, even
at home, when brought face to face with
the needs of the human soul. What we
commonly detect among Chinese missioners
we find in the subject of this memoir. Quite
naturally he is being transformed as it were,
his spirit is already intoxicated with holy
zeal; he is in fact fast growing out of the
ordinary humdrum priest into the uncon-
scious hero of self-immolation. This pheno-
menon (not, as we said, rare among the
missioners of the Far East) we cannot
presume quite to explain—but as a matter
of fact, the atmosphere seems to be charged,
to contain an exhilaration like that found
by the mountain-climber when he has
reached the summit.

When Father Moloney left Paris, was
he not an ordinary student—a good one,
of course? If he had remained at home
in all probability he would have thought
and spoken and written like an ordinary
person. Now, it comes to him quite naturally and without a trace of affectation to
say that one fine day he may be butchered
(as he knew his countrywoman, Alice
O'Sullivan, had been butchered only four
years previously), but that it makes no

matter to him! He has been plunged into these pagan surroundings, he has been steeped in their all-pervading atmosphere, fœtid, human, appalling to his Christian sense. On the other hand, his compeers— they, like him, have burned their boats, they, like him, are in the constant presence of danger, of death, of sin, of ignorance, of vile superstition. They, like him, see human and divine things with opened eyes; they, like him, can pierce the veil; their souls, like his, have been stung with a sense of contrast; their lives are lived upon a higher plane, their pulses are quickened with a nobler faith, an intenser desire to draw near to the Crucified.

Thus we may easily surmise that this double environment of a young missioner —Paganism pressing on him close and Christian heroism pressing on him closer still—does to some extent account for a change in his outlook, almost in his very nature. Like another missioner, Patrick even in the year 1874, could say, "No longer I live, but Christ liveth in me."

When we read an account of the early Christian neophytes, in the times of persecution, when we think of them living their life, not knowing each day whether it were their last, we can quite understand that they took very little count of those trifles that we imagine to be important. Spiritual things were to them real, because

they were eternal. They were bound together in a common danger, they were
united against a common foe, they viewed
their lives from a common standpoint.

If we compare to such a standard the life
lived in China by the missionaries at Father
Moloney's arrival in the seventies, it will not
be impossible for us to realise that even in
his third year he had begun to imbibe the
heroic spirit and that it now came natural
to him to adopt language which, if used by
one of ourselves, might appear exaggerated.
Anyhow he wrote those things.

Those who have read the letters have
learned something about the downright
character, what we have called the heroism of the writer, and also they can understand why he was regarded with no little
admiration and affection by his Chinese
converts. Père Dauverchain tells us he
had entirely won their hearts, and it is
credible. The Chinese are not an emotional
race, but they are by no means wanting in
intuition, nor are they ungrateful. On the
contrary, those who know them best aver
that they are warm-hearted and disposed
to reciprocate goodness wherever they find
it. It is, indeed a very remarkable fact that
European missionaries, whether priests or
nuns, become strongly attached to the
Chinese, and even speak of them, in spite
of their many undoubted faults, as a high-
minded and chivalrous race.

FATHER MOLONEY IN HIS CHINESE COSTUME

CHAPTER XI

MARTYR OF CHARITY

THE reader might like to have further details of Father Patrick's missionary labours, but in reality there was probably not very much to record. Or shall we say that the less there was to record upon earth, the more of his work is recorded in heaven ? Humanly speaking his life was excessively uninteresting, one month being much the same as the others, with very little excitement except such as is inherent in the quest for human souls.

There is, however, one letter we should like the reader to see before coming on to the closing scenes of a short and uneventful career. It seems pathetic when we know the circumstances in which it was written.

On October 10th, 1881, only three months before his death, he wrote it from Kiou-Kiang, "to all my dearest brothers and sisters," giving a most vivid description of his labours, "just to give you an idea of our position, and also of the vigorous health of your humble servant," evidently with no thought that it would be his last letter home. He says :—

" It is about two years since I last wrote ;

8　　　113

ever since I have been on different missions.
Everywhere I see and speak with pagans,
they are always curious to see me, and I
am ever ready to exhibit myself to them,
and speak with them on their eternal wel-
fare . . . I will be in Kiang-si ten years
next December, and during this time more
than 50,000 pagan children have been
baptised at the hour of death. Now, I will
tell you about a sick-call I got last June.
I had more than seventy miles to go to it.
I set out on the 12th of the month, and
walked twenty miles that day. I was to
get a small boat for the rest of the journey,
but contrary winds prevented our crossing
a famous lake called the Po-yang-hon.

"On the 13th I left on foot, as the wind did
not permit me to go in a boat. After travelling six miles I had to return, as I could
not cross a river. On the 14th I tried a
boat, but could not go ahead. On the 15th,
fearing the patient might die, I went by
land, and travelled fifteen miles. On the
16th I walked thirty miles. On the 17th
it was raining, and the roads were covered
with the mountain torrents in several
places. I walked in some places with the
water, and about noon I arrived, drenched
with perspiration and covered with mud,
at a miserable eating.house, where I had
to remain two nights. I walked twelve
miles that day. Those two days were very
painful to me, as I had still to cross a lake,

and no boat could do it, and I was afraid
the sick person would die before I reached
her. However, I reached the end of my
journey about 4 p.m. on the 20th, and the
sick woman was still alive. Having admin-
istered the Sacraments to her, I was back
to my ordinary duties on the 24th of June.
Very often I walk from twenty to thirty
miles a day. A walk of 12 to 15 miles is
only a recreation, and I doubt if any of you
could surpass the Chinaman in walking."

We shall now proceed to give a short
account of Father Moloney's death, as it
is described by his Bishop.

At Easter, in the year 1875, he had
been designated by the unanimous desire
of the Episcopal Council for a post of
great difficulty in a part of the Vicariate,
which was later erected, by the separation
of Kiang-si, into a pro-vicariate apostolic.
There was some question even at the later
date, of entrusting the work of organising
the new ecclesiastical centre to the young
Irish missionary, and his name was sent to
Rome; but as he was only thirty-eight
the office fell to the lot of another, and
Father Moloney was transferred to take
the place of his brother priest, on whose
shoulders the choice of the Holy See had
placed a new and heavy burden.

At this time many Europeans had fallen
victims to a dangerous form of dysentery,
and our countryman was among those

who were attacked.   His life was again
spared, and he now spent a whole year at
Kien-Shang, after which it became necessary to recall him to Kiou-Kiang, to be
again placed under the care of the Scotch
physician, whose treatment of his former
complaint had proved so successful.   Finding himself once more in a state of perfect
health, he burned with zeal to return to
the mission he had left.

Mgr. Bray relates at this time he found
him filled with the deepest humility, yet
often and often he would come to his (the
Bishop's) own room, and exclaim, "Ecce
ego, mitte me "—" When shall it be permitted me to start ?"   On the Feast of the
Immaculate Conception, in the year 1881,
he was despatched to Yao-tcheou, where
there were a number of Christian settle-
ments which required to be stirred up to
new fervour.   Meanwhile, Mgr.   Bray
quitted Kiou-Kiang, and went to Kiang-si,
which he did not reach till the end of
January.   On his arrival he heard that
news had come of Father Moloney's serious
illness.   He had been struck down by a
kind of virulent cancer (called in Chinese
Ting-tsang), which frequently proved
quickly fatal, especially if it was in the
head, and on the left side.   The particulars
of Father Moloney's case were not stated,
and a priest had started off in hot haste on a
long journey to bring him the consola-

tions of religion, but it was feared the
sufferer might be dead before his arrival.
We will now give the Bishop's own words :

"My God, what a miserable week I
passed ! On the 7th of February, after
finishing the *Maria Mater Gratiae* of night
prayers, I saw a man come to throw himself
at my feet. It was the priest who had come
back. All I could say was, ' Well ? ' ' Yes,'
he replied. 'Monseigneur, God has asked
from us a great sacrifice.' ' Is he dead ? '
' Yes, on the 22nd, after five days of fright-
ful pain.' "

The Bishop then goes on to relate how
successfully Father Moloney had been conducting his mission. He had been baptising several adults, and receiving catechumens in different places, and had,
moreover, persuaded some military men
to embrace the faith. After the disease
appeared in his face, he continued to travel
from place to place, notwithstanding the
protests of the Christians, till in the end
he could go no further, and had to lie down
to die. He had with him as a Mass-server,
a native who had been formerly a pupil
in the *petit seminaire*. He stated that no
less than nine doctors inspected him, all
of whom declared that his complaint was
incurable. The patient displayed the most
perfect resignation, spending his time in
making acts of contrition and conformity
to the will of God, and in invoking the

sacred names of Jesus, Mary, Joseph, and
St. Vincent, of whose congregation he was
a member. Even when he appeared to be
delirious, he kept reciting the *Ave Maris
Stella,* the *Ave Joseph,* etc.

The Christians, according to their wont
in such cases, made for his intention the
Stations of the Cross. The writer says that
during ten years of his episcopal experience he knew this devotion to be carried on
in similar cases, and always with the result
of some improvement in the sick person
for whom it was done. In the case of
Father Moloney the effect on him was,
that he saw white flowers on one side of
the room, and red ones on the other, and
in the midst a fair child, who asked which
flowers he would choose—the white or the
red ? He replied : " I care not, only what
the good God wills." Mgr. Bray adds,
that he repeats the story to show the
resignation of the dying priest.

After this he could not speak or even arti-
culate the holy names, which were whispered
into his ears by the faithful attendant, and
he died exactly at four o'clock the following
morning. Thus, like his prototype St.
Francis Xavier, he died all but alone with
God. Who that believes in God will pity him ?

The good Bishop writes that he felt
almost heart-broken at the sudden and
unexpected death of so young and efficient
a subject. He adds that Father Moloney

had been a man of great physical strength, and endowed with a good constitution, as his past history had proved. His character was naturally quick, and even hasty ; but he had learned to exercise such self-control that he was regarded as particularly amiable, and was, indeed, most beloved by all who had any dealings with him. He possessed the spirit of rule and of fidelity to his vocation to a high degree, was blessed with a great gift of prayer, and was specially devout to the Most Holy Sacrament and to the ever Blessed Virgin.

Monseigneur Bray closes this interesting memoir with an apology for the hurried way in which it was necessarily composed, and asks that the Superior of the Irish College, to whom it is written, may communicate with Father Moloney's family, who will, he thinks, be delighted that their relative, called after the Apostle of Ireland, was worthy of such a father ; and that, having lived such a life of zeal and holy charity, he had died, with his arms in his hands, as a brave soldier of the cross. We will go a little further than the writer of the letter, and will venture to express a hope that it may stir up the souls of Catholic Irish parents to dedicate their sons to a life—aye, and, if God should so will, to a death—like that of Patrick Moloney, apostle and martyr of charity. " Moriatur anima mea morte justorum."

CHAPTER XII

IT is singularly appropriate that the two
preceding lives should be completed by a
short account of another Tipperary Sister,
who went to the Chinese Mission at the call
of Father Moloney, her near kinsman, and
who lived for years, and was buried, under
the shadow of the little church where are
preserved the charred relics of the Martyr
of Clonmel.

Mary Ryan was born a few miles from
Cashel on the Eve of Epiphany, 1851, and
entered the Vincentian Order in May, 1872.
Her father was brother to Father Patrick
Moloney's mother. We have already given,
on page 106, the letter written to her by her
cousin two years later on the occasion of
her religious profession. She was for several
years on the Mission at Lanark, and in
London, but was in constant correspondence
with Father Patrick, and, though she had
long been anxiously desirous to follow him
to his strange and distant mission, when
at length her wishes were realised, it was
only to hear of his early and unexpected
death in the same year as she arrived in
China, 1882. This resolution can hardly

120

have surprised her family, nor do they
appear to have offered any opposition to
it, though it must certainly have caused
them a pang to separate for ever from one
who was so universally and deservedly
loved. Like other members of her family,
many of whom have been and are priests
and religious, and one of whom was among
the most widely esteemed priests of the
diocese of Cashel, and for years on the staff
of clergy serving the Cathedral Church,
Mary Ryan had been from earliest childhood remarkable for her sterling qualities
and spirit of genuine piety. It is related
by one who owes much to her that when
a mere girl she used to spend hours praying,
and often stopped up at night for the purpose. Moreover, living a long distance
from a church, she would climb a neighbouring hill whence she could descry the
cathedral spire at a distance of seven miles,
and would then pour out her heart to Our
Lord whose Presence was therein taber-
nacled. Her immediate preparation for
conventual life was gained from the residence in her father's house of a brother
who had been recently ordained, and who
did his best to encourage her in her desire
to consecrate herself to the service of God.

With such antecedents it is not to be
wondered at that Sister Vincent, as we may
now call her, threw herself heart and soul
into the work she had, by God's grace,

chosen as her " better part." She laboured
in China for sixteen years, and though for
several years before her death, which
occurred on December 3rd (the feast of St.
Francis Xavier), 1898, she had been a great
sufferer from disease of the heart, yet she
did not relax her efforts till about six or
seven weeks before the end. Her death
was undoubtedly accelerated by a carriage
accident, in which she was upset and badly
shaken, although she declared herself that
she was not hurt (nor was she externally).
This happened about the middle of October.
She had gone to Pekin to make her annual
retreat early in the month, and it was in
returning to Tien-tsin that the carriage was
overturned, and very soon after she felt
that her death was at hand. On the day
on which it occurred she said it was her
last, but that she would live till evening,
which was the case.

Writing after the event, her Superior
wrote of her :—

" This dear Sister has certainly won a
bright crown for herself by her piety and
her untiring devotion to the poor and
afflicted. Last summer, though her limbs
were swollen, and she was in such miserable
health, yet she was on her feet nearly all
day, waiting on the poor Chinese, or the
European patients, never sparing herself.
The doctors said her courage was marvellous; the same may be said of her

patience and resignation during the two
months she was confined to the infirmary.
Her poor legs were swollen to an enormous
size, water flowed from them abundantly ;
she was not able to move, and God only
knows what she suffered, no doubt in order
that, being purified from all stains, her soul
might pass from earth to the everlasting
joys of heaven."

The writer of this little notice has been
able, by the kindness of a brother of the
devoted nun, to peruse a large number of
letters written by her at various times
during her sojourn among the Chinese.
Many of them are too personal, too sacred,
for the general public ; but we cannot altogether miss the opportunity offered ; hoping
that a few extracts laid before the readers,
especially those of her own county, may
warm their hearts to try at least in some
way to imitate the devotion of this remarkable member of the trio of Tipperary
missioners.

Writing in 1892 from Kiang-si, she says :
" You must have heard of the massacre
of Christians in Mongolia, and how the
Emperor sent a cord to the Mandarin in
charge, with which he executed himself, as
is customary in China, in grave offences
against His Majesty. We are very quiet
here ; all the troubles seem over. Fearing
you might be anxious about me, I give you
this sign of life, though I am not in writing

humour. I am looking after a patient that is nearly crushed. . . . I caught cold at the midnight Mass in the church, and was obliged to remain in bed about twelve days (I am only just out of it) with an attack of jaundice and rheumatism, with which my heart foolishly harmonised."

Later in the same letter, of which only a fragment is preserved, she says: " Friday next will be the tenth anniversary of Father Moloney's death ; " and, speaking of a letter from her sister, she adds: " I received it in bed, and it seemed to make my heart better directly. Dear Kate, perhaps I shall soon hear of her reception."

In 1893 she wrote, from Kiu-Kiang, Kiang-si, referring to the same sister, after she had been professed :—

" Surely Our Lord will accept of her as His servant, and a good one I think she will make. How I love the motto *Ecce Ancilla Domini*, higher titles don't suit such as the Spouse of the Lord, because I feel too small for it, but I rejoice in the Little Servant of the Lord " (the above is in French). " I speak very little English now, but feel quite at home in French ; even Chinese is getting pretty natural at present. I am, thank God, very well, in fact very strong, but just at present very sad, as we have lost a kind, good Sister Superior. Poor thing, she died of fever only eight days ago. We had great anxiety for three

weeks, and great fatigue, as she was very
ill from the first. Her death, like her life,
was calm and edifying. I seldom left her
in the day, and at night we both took our
turn. She is a great loss to us. We made
our noviciate in Paris together, and now
it fell to my lot to close her eyes on the
banks of the Yang-tse after 21 years. She
is here only 16 months, but is seven years
in China. R.I.P."

Writing to her brother on his ordination,
in 1896, she says :—

" I do not expect that Our Lord will free
you altogether from troubles, as it would
not be good for you, as you would only
lose a great means of sanctification. These
troubles were sent you to purify and
chasten your heart, so that, when the
long-wished-for hour of prostrating yourself on the altar-steps arrives, you may be
almost as pure as the day I held you in
my arms at the baptismal font, which I
remember very well. How I would love to
be present at your ordination ! But *fiat* in
all things. I have seen several ordained in
China, as the Vincentians and others come
out to finish here, and to study the language
at the same time, which gives them sooner
to this needful mission, where labourers
are so few."

And, later in the year, on the same
subject :—

" Your blessing, please ; yes, and a double

one I want also ! in the quality of mother
and sister. My own dearest brother, blessed
be God, you are a priest. What gratitude
we owe to God and to our Immaculate
Mother to have brought you to this happy
day, the 21st of June, twelfth anniversary
of poor mother's death ! Yes, thrice-blessed
and happy day for you and all of us. Our
lives will be too short to prove our gratitude
by devoting ourselves lovingly in God's
service ; but we shall continue through all
eternity, shall we not ? . . . Fear not ; throw
yourself right into the mission ; preach,
instruct, and exhort. I can imagine Kate's
delight to see you at the altar, and all the
others are, no doubt, in the joy of their
hearts. I need not ask a memento and a
Mass sometimes for my intentions (my first
two are the Sisters at Tien-tsin and at
Kiu-Kiang), and a Young Priest's blessing.
I got Pat's in a hotel in Dublin, and John's
in London, in August, '93. I can imagine
Mother Angela's pride. It is your turn to
preach to me, as you are a priest of the
Church of God, and I am only ' an exile in
the Land of Martyrs.'"

Writing later in the same year, to the
same, from Tien-tsin, she says, in reference
to the martyrs of 1870, for one of whom she
naturally felt such a strong affection :—

"We are rejoicing at present here. The
first glimpse of glory has come for the
martyrs of 1870. The Emperor has ordered,

and given means to the Bishop to rebuild
the Church of Our Lady of Victories, and
erect a royal monument on the grounds.
The work has begun. A German Bishop
told us a few days ago that several of the
bishops have asked for the canonisation
of the missioners and sisters."

And in the following year also from
Tien-tsin :—

" I promised to give you an account of
our Feast, 21st June, but in reality I saw
little of it, except through visits of the
Fathers who came for the Feast. It was
carried out in an official, but very quiet
manner, as they feared trouble from the
secret societies, who saw with anger the
church they destroyed 27 years restored,
and a royal monument beside it, declaring
the innocence of the victims of 1870, and
also that the government and people had
no hand in it, but only the revolutionists.
The grand white marble monument is
placed so near the river that all who pass
by can read it. The two missionaries and
what remained of the sisters and four
secular gentlemen and two ladies were
moved ; ' the coffins ' were taken into the
Church and placed in vaults with a grand
marble slab in the wall over each, the
missionaries and sisters at one side and the
seculars at the other. I will go there in a
few days, and I will pray for each of those
so dear to my heart. Tell Mat that I expect

him if possible to say Mass for me on the 14th September, which will be my silver jubilee. Only fancy how old I am, though I am (when I am not ill) taken for 35 instead of 46."

And here we leave Mary Ryan, and her work for China.

But will *Tipperary's Gift to China* also end here?

THE END

CPSIA information can be obtained at www.ICGtesting.com
Printed in the USA
LVOW13*1245230314

378556LV00005B/65/P